The Router Book

The Router Book

A Complete Guide to the Router and Its Accessories

Pat Warner

The Taunton Press

The Taunton Press
Inspiration for hands-on living™

The Taunton Press, Inc., 63 South Main Street, P.O. Box 5506, Newtown, CT 06470-5506
e-mail: tp@taunton.com

Distributed by Publishers Group West

INTERIOR DESIGN: Mary McKeon
LAYOUT: Rosalie Vaccaro
ILLUSTRATOR: Ron Carboni
COVER PHOTOGRAPHY: Scott Phillips
INTERIOR PHOTOGRAPHY: Lon Atkinson

LIBRARY OF CONGRESS CATALOGING-IN-PUBLICATION DATA
Warner, Pat, 1943-
    The router book / Pat Warner.
        p. cm.
    ISBN 1-56158-423-1
    1. Routers (Tools) 2. Woodwork. I. Title.

TT203.5 .W3735 2001
684'.08--dc21   2001027149

Printed in the United States of America
10 9 8 7 6 5 4 3 2 1

To my wife, Judy Ann, without whom this work would still be a pile of dusty, handwritten folders.

Acknowledgments

I had plenty of help on this book. Please let me thank Jürgen Amtmann for his engineering expertise; Nathan Detroit for his computer skills; Phil Stivers for his excellent woodwork in preparing the materials for the inlay photos; Alan Goodsel and Carlos Venditto for their router bit expertise; Pat Spielman, Strother Purdy, Todd Langston and Jeff Stoltz of Porter-Cable; John Treacy of Wetzler Clamp; Chris Carlson of Bosch; Barry Rundstrom; Frank Kunkel; Gary Rogowski; John Goff; Dave Keller; Richard Wedler; and Eric Johnson.

ABOUT YOUR SAFETY

Working with wood is inherently dangerous. Using hand or power tools improperly or ignoring safety practices can lead to permanent injury or even death. Don't try to perform operations you learn about here (or elsewhere) unless you're certain they are safe for you. If something about an operation doesn't feel right, don't do it. Look for another way. We want you to enjoy the craft, so please keep safety foremost in your mind whenever you're in the shop.

Contents

Introduction

What I like most about routing is the ability to manage risk. I know that with the right cutters, jigs and fixtures I can remove the right amount of wood in the right place. The ability to do this does not happen overnight, however. Practice, respect for the material, attention to cutter dynamics and good fixtures all play a part.

Routers are the big time problem solvers of the power tool kingdom. They have more applications than any single cutting tool. They apply themselves well in joinery, decoration, and in a limited way, millwork. More than 1,000 cutters, and countless jigs are at your disposal for almost any routing job.

Nevertheless, routing does have its limitations. Spend some time with this book and you will discover the practical limits and also the strengths of routing. Just reading the book won't make you into an expert router user, but a lot of practice will. Expect to finish this text and walk away with the fundamentals of the craft: how to choose a cutter and router, when to apply them, when to consider an alternative, and how to use the tool safely.

Introduction to Routing

Routers have worked themselves into the premiere spot among woodworking power tools—only drills outsell them among portable power tools. It's even fairly common for woodworkers to own a small family of routers in different sizes and shapes. But the sheer size of the router field can make the job of choosing the right tool seem daunting. And the vast number of accessories on the market offers a feast of choices that provides another challenge. To navigate this sea of choices, and find a sound strategy to incorporate this tool in our shops, we might think about why we use these tools to begin with and what makes them so special.

This pair of experimental round tenons demonstrates the measured and precise removal of material. The tenons are part of the stock; they are not dowels.

The author's mortising jig uses a pair of edge guides and a pair of jig stops so it can be adjusted to rout virtually any mortise.

Routing is basically the high-speed removal of stock from a workpiece; think of it as the measured wasting of material. All sorts of materials can be routed, but solid wood may be the most common. And while the tool has many uses other than woodworking, most router bits are designed primarily for use with wood and plywood. However, medium-density fiberboard (MDF), plastic, solid-surface material—even rock or metal—can be routed given enough power, the right setup, and appropriate tooling. But the majority of us work with wood most often.

Many woodworking processes, including routing, are subtractive. I can't think of an example where routing adds anything to a workpiece. In many forms of art, such as ceramics and goldsmithing, the material is reformed and added to the whole, thus conserving materials. Not so with wood: We chop, saw, sand, drill, plane, joint, and rout most of our resource away. And routers are the preeminent stock removers. They can remove stock on the edge, on the ends of a workpiece, or anywhere in the middle. And they can remove stock in nearly any profile, from a thin slice along the edge for jointing, to complex shapes for raised panels, cope-and-stick joinery, or decorative details. Depending on the power and size, they can remove the tiny burr of plastic laminate while trimming a countertop or hog out a mortise in hard maple. So as we investigate router choices in subsequent chapters, a major consideration will always be the scope of the work and the power requirements.

Routing is rarely done to rough stock. Routers normally are used after the jointer, planer, and table saw operations. That is one of their distinctions. They can't—or shouldn't—compete with tools that prepare stock. They are intended for precision work. This will be taken into account as we discuss the various choices.

But routers, unlike many hand tools, need jigs, fixtures, fences, and holders to apply themselves. Edge and collar guides, custom subbases and various kinds of templates are very useful. But even more important are the jigs, fixtures, and platforms that provide a way to do precise joinery. The router is seriously handicapped without its accessories. You can rout with bearing-guided profile cutters without much ado, but virtually any

This ensemble is not cheap, by any stretch, but for a lifetime woodworker they will cover most routing challenges. From left: DeWalt 621 plunge router, PC-690 mid-range fixed base router, 310-PC trim router, PC-7518 fixed base router.

Fluting, whether on flat stock or mounted on a lathe, is one of the router's important uses.

Finish carpenters typically use routers to mortise for hinges on custom door installations.

Trim routers may get their heaviest use in countertop fabrication. Here, plastic laminate is being flush-trimmed after being glued down on the particleboard substrate.

other cut (without bearings) will require some jig, fixture or external guide. Another consideration, then, is the router's ability to work well with a variety of jigs and fixtures.

Because of their great and vast potential, routers are major woodworking problem solvers. No other tool finds its way into so many facets of woodworking. Routers apply themselves well in the joinery and decoration of your work, excel in making jigs, fixtures and templates, and—even better—they can usually help you out of a jam. They are, it's true, dependent on a massive array of potential jigs, fixtures, holders and cutters but they also help solve nearly every woodworking problem. No other tool offers so many cutting and shaping possibilities. And no other tool provides quite the same challenge when it comes to sorting through all the choices to get the right tooling to match your particular needs.

Applications

So far we've talked about the router's use for a variety of woodworking tasks, its relationship to other tools, its array of accessories, and the way it can reach any part of the workpiece. Let's take a minute and talk about the most important criterion of them all, the router's specific applications. The router has three major areas of application: decoration, joinery, and millwork.

TYPES OF ROUTING

Type	Description	Duty Cycle	Power Demand (hp)	Router
Light-trim	Flush trim laminate/veneer. Shallow, small cutter routing	Short	< 1	Trim router
Decorative trim, light-duty edge	Shallow edge cuts up to ⅜ in. x ⅜ in. Volume, ogees, bevels, ball bearing decorator and template cuts.	0–60 minutes	1½–2 router	Medium fixed-base
Plunge	Inside multistage work, large excavations; casting must be supported for plunge. Mortises, circles and laps.	Can be long	1½–3 will be acceptable for most work	Plunge router
Table	All stationary work.	No time limit	3+	Fixed-base or plunge router (more common)
Heavy-duty hand router	Edge and template full-thickness cuts.	All day	3+	Big fixed-base
Template	Pattern work; line, fractional or full thickness cuts.	No time limit	1–3	All routers and tables

DECORATION

Categorically, the greatest number of router bits are for trim and decoration. Catalog inventories usually exceed 50 percent in decorator cutters. This is strange in a way, because decoration has so little to do with practicality; your desk, jewelry box, or bed will survive just as well without decoration. Nevertheless, finishing and decoration are two of the most important criteria in which woodwork is judged. It would indeed be a mistake to overlook them.

JOINERY

The power of the router is in its joint-making capability. Nearly all of Western joinery is possible with a router, with the addition of its cutters, jigs and you. It has its limitations, like bridle joints and deep skinny dovetails, but it can address an enormous number of both ordinary and special joints. But the router isn't perfect, and there are many occasions, due to fixturing, cutter design and so on that a joint is compromised. You may not exceed or even meet the capacities of a hand joiner, but do expect to make mortises and tenons; tongues and grooves; laps; glue joints; through, blind, and sliding dovetails; splines; lock miters; cope and stick; box joints; and various combinations.

This screw-driven router fence employs a dial indicator to achieve accuracy in the thousandths of an inch range.

This platform jig uses an oversized base and a ball bearing rabbeting bit to form a square tenon on the end of a workpiece.

Routing lends itself well to a wide range of joinery challenges.

MILLWORK

Router work that doesn't fall into the decoration or joinery genres I call millwork. This is not the millwork associated with shapers and molders. Rather, it is work like trimming panels to length, jointing, dimensioning, and squaring stock. I also use the router to make jigs, and I frequently make short runs of jigs and fixtures for those of you who'd rather wood-work. The platforms and their windows are usually template routed. The squared fences, adjustable slots, and rabbeted stops are also routed.

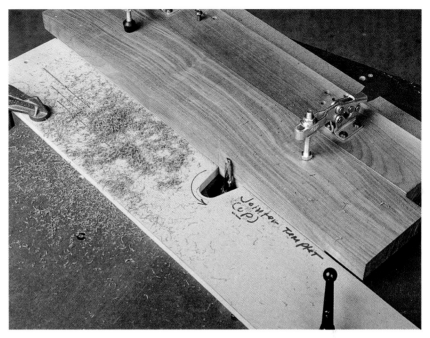

Wide glue-ups pose serious dimensioning problems. A jigsaw, router, and template can be used to square off the ends.

The fence on the work holder can be adjusted parallel to its work edge. With the cutter surrounded by an MDF straight fence, you can joint and machine to width in one operation.

Inexpensive router bits can reproduce a variety of traditional profiles.

Types of Routing

It would be a mistake to think that all of this application can be enjoyed with just one router. It can't be done. There are some cuttings that, if done to full depth, will break the cutter; sometimes the router is just too small and underpowered for the job. Certain cuts put the work or the operator at risk with the wrong router. There are problems of scale that may require the router table. Small jobs may be better suited for a trim router, and multistage work should be done with a plunge router. However, routing is versatile and there are distinctions you should know about.

LIGHT TRIM

Frequently, trade work calls for very light and shallow cuts in wood, metal, or plastic. These cuts are of short duration, and require little power or set-up complexity. You may not need a full-size router for these cuts. Examples include the mortising of hinges, chamfering, and small roundovers. But mostly I'm talking about the cutting and trimming of plastic laminate (Formica), wood veneers, fiberglass and thin aluminum. This work is always light duty, shallow, done with only 1/4-in. tool shanks, and only with trim routers.

The PC-310 trimmer and offset subbase are a good match to trim (bevel) these edges. The work can be seen through the plastic base while the router is kept flat on the work.

Sliding dovetails are great for locking legs and rails. Sockets are made on the router table and the tenons with the hand router.

Bread and butter trim (cove) cuts require about 1.5 hp, a sharp cutter, and a medium-weight fixed base.

DECORATIVE TRIM

The next level of complexity I call decorative trim. Work is of medium duration (up to 30 minutes or so) along the edge of stock or template, and the fixed single-depth cuts are less than the equivalent of a ⅜-in. by ⅜-in. groove. These cuts are too demanding for a trim router and not enough for an industrial-strength tool. Some fixturing may be required, but most of the work is decorative, using bearing-guided trim cutters like ogees, roundovers, rabbets, and bevels. This work is best done with midrange fixed-base routers typically of 1 hp to 2 hp. The fixed base is low-centered, close-handled, and has a small casting designed for this kind of work.

A big cut like a slice off the face of this tenon requires a lot of power. The weight of this tool may be a safety factor rather than a control problem.

HEAVY-DUTY HAND ROUTING

The cuttings in this category are often all-day, fixed-depth cuts like big single-pass roundovers, dovetails, dadoes, and full-thickness template cuts for sink cutouts or furniture parts. These cuts are also along the edge of the stock or template. This is hand routing at its finest. Midsized routers "stumble" when called for this duty. Big cutters are common, $\frac{3}{4}$ in. to $1\frac{1}{2}$ in. in diameter and up to $1\frac{3}{4}$ in. long. Fixtures, templates, and jigs are more common than ball-bearing profile bits. The cuts are often more than $\frac{3}{8}$ in. by $\frac{3}{8}$ in. or as deep as the design of the cutter and power will permit. Again, this is the domain of the fixed-base router, not for stability but because these cuts are essentially single pass-single depth and do not use the multistage capability of the plunge router. In this case, the cutter is set to depth and not changed. Some shops buy dedicated single-cut routers for this work.

PLUNGE ROUTING

Routers designed to allow changes in depth without shutting off the machine have come to be called plunge routers. The base incorporates a mechanism with a series of stops so that the router can be lowered incrementally. The design allows you, for example, to quickly rout a deep mortise in a number of smaller steps that only remove ¼ in. or so of material at a time. It also allows you to start a cut anywhere in the middle of a workpiece—and it is especially useful when routing on panels.

Although it's possible to "plunge" a fixed-base router into the work, it's an inherently unsafe operation because the base isn't supported during the operation. Plunging is simply not safe with a fixed-base router. The plunge

Mortises and tenons require fixtures for quality and repeatability. A good fit like this imposes a lot of demands on the jigs.

Half-laps are shallow and large in area, perfect for the plunge router. These are made in a template jig (under the work).

router is expressly designed to function in your hands with the aid of gravity. Its spring-load motor head, turret stops, upstop, handle grips, motor lock and switch are all situated for you to slide the tool to its destination with the cutter retracted and motor on. Now, with you at the controls, you can safely change the depth under power and waste wood in stages.

The plunge router does its best work "plunging." Plunging is best carried out and sometimes only possible when the router is completely sur-

Tongues and grooves of all sorts can be made on the router table with straight bits.

Stopped open mortises are safely done on the router table.

rounded by substrate. Plunging with only half of the casting on the work can tip the router over or, in some cases, arrest the plunge action altogether. The safest arena for plunging then is on inside cuts like mortises. That is not to say that plunge routing cannot be along the edges and ends of the workpiece. It just means that the base casting has to be on solid ground to support its plunging function and relative top heaviness. Cuttings that are deep and wide or otherwise impossible with a single-depth setting should be done with a plunge router. Plunge cuts too dangerous for a fixed-base router also include inside blind excavations where the cutter must be under power and extended to begin the pass.

TABLE ROUTING

Table routing essentially turns the tool into a stationary machine with a fence that wraps around the cutter and supports the workpiece. Unlike portable routing operations, the workpiece moves past the cutter, instead of the reverse. More than 80 percent of all routing can be done on the router table. There are restrictions to its use (such as very large work and long sticks on end) but the majority of routing is on individual workpieces and quite manageable on the table.

Router table work, more often than not, demands a lot of power. There is no single router tailored exclusively for the router table. Big motors, resistant to changes in momentum and load, are required here. Long-grain, cross-grain, end-cutting, and some inside cuts are possible on the table. Joinery and template work are also common. (Only use very long cutters over 1¾ in. These cutters require at least a 3-hp motor and work best with variable speed control.)

Complementary template joinery is about the only way to join wood along curvy lines. One sample is a lap, left, one is glue jointed, middle, and the other is tongue and groove, top.

I use these templates to make the platform for the tenon-maker. Since the instructions are already "carved" into the template, you can't make a mistake.

TEMPLATE ROUTING

Template routing allows you to rout multiples of nearly any shape by using a pattern that's attached to the workpiece and rides against a guide pin or other reference surface. Templates can be used for joinery, making copies, mortising, shaping, and making parts for jigs. Most repetitive routing jobs can be expedited by a template.

By far, the most popular type of cutter in my router locker is the pattern bit with a bearing on top. These come in many diameters and lengths for use in a variety of situations. The art of template routing demands an

THERE ARE A HOST OF ACCESSORIES available to extend the capabilities of your router. There are, for example, aftermarket subbases made from clear plastic (at lower left above) that will allow greater visibility as you're making a pass with the router. Also available are subbases with an offset design (upper left) that provide greater control because more of the base is on the workpiece as you work.

Another category of accessories is the edge guide, which acts much like the fence of a table saw and rides along the edge of workpiece (upper right). The two at top are shop-made edge guides; the black guide in the middle is an aftermarket edge guide made by Micro Fence (see Resources on p. 180).

There are also a variety of collar guides (lower right) to fit most popular routers. The collar guides fit into the subbase and surround the bit, providing a way for the cut to follow a template.

understanding of all forms of routing, guide systems, clamping procedures, jig making, and basic woodworking. Template routing can be done on the table or on the bench with plunge or fixed base. It is the essence of routing.

Just as no single knife will work in the kitchen, no single router will suffice for all routing applications. Trying to cover all bases with one router will have you overpowered in one situation and at risk in another—or perhaps empty-handed if the router is tied up in the router table. Just as the jigsaw, radial saw, table saw, and bandsaw address your sawing needs, so do the trim, plunge, medium and heavy fixed-base router cover your routing needs.

Cutter Pathway Control

How well you control the pathway of the router bit determines the quality of your results. There is more to routing than cutter control, but without it you have nothing. Cutter quality, material preparation, feed rate, setup and attention to detail all play a part in the quality of your cuttings—but without control of the cutter pathway, you'll never get to practice the finer points of routing.

A router can move in a straight line or on a radius. It has trouble routing in three axes at the same time. Scooping chair seats or making globes is not an easy task with a router, and very sophisticated engineering and fixturing is required to do so. Hand control of the router, whether in a curved or straight path, in one plane at a time, can be established with cutter bearings, collars, pivots, edge guides, templates, and various combinations.

As mentioned, routers are very flexible tools and can, unlike a table or band saw, operate as easily in the middle of a workpiece as on an edge. The router bit can enter from any surface, either face, any edge, either end, or along the radius of a curve. The cut can be blind, enter from the edge and stop inside (half-blind), or pass right through it. This much freedom does require precise guide systems, but this may not to be as daunting as it appears.

A router guide can be as simple as a board clamped onto the workpiece. There are many ways to control the router. These vary from the built-in controls and basic edge guides to micrometer-controlled circle guides and even computerized positioning devices that are outside the scope of this book. But for discussion purposes, it's probably best to start at the center of things, with the various ways the bit itself can guide the work at hand.

Bearing on Top

Top-bearing-guided cutters, or pattern bits, are always used with a template.

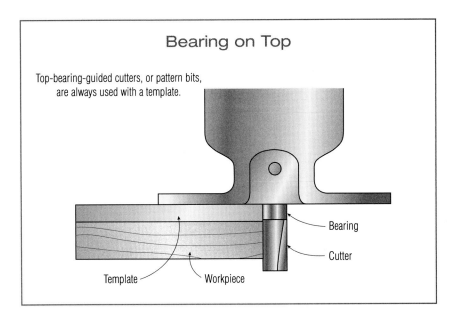

Bearing

Cutter

Template

Workpiece

Bearing on Bottom

End-bearing cutters typically roll along the workpiece.

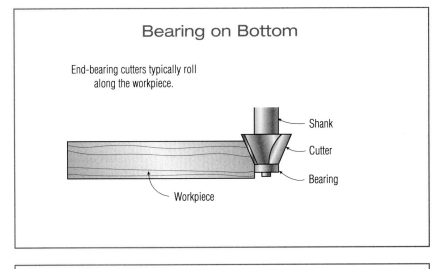

Shank

Cutter

Bearing

Workpiece

Collar Guide System

A typical collar-guide system uses a template and a smaller bit so that the cutting path is offset from the template.

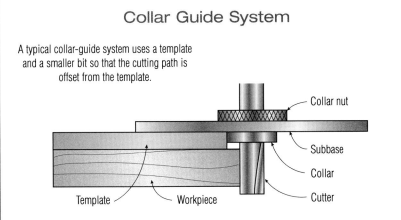

Collar nut

Subbase

Collar

Cutter

Template

Workpiece

CHART OF GUIDE SYSTEMS

ADVANTAGES	DISADVANTAGES
Collar Inexpensive; safe; allows just enough cutter extension; inside cuts possible; can be used with any cutter less than 1-in. diameter; easy on router.	Sensitive to edge defects; eccentric, inaccurate; often requires modification; maximum cutter useful = 1-in. diameter; template compensation (offset) required; must make templates; full cutter extension not possible; incremental, not continuous adjustment.
Bottom Bearing Low skill demand; very accurate, simple; can work on assemblies or installations in the field.	Wears out fast; mars the work; hard on router bearings/sensitive to edge defects; cutters are bigger, expensive, usually restricted to cut one radius; can't be used on inside cuts; increments only, no continuous adjustment.
Steel Pilot Very cheap, can get into tight corners.	Burns wood; sensitive to edge defects.
Shank Bearing Tools Can be used on almost any bit; maximum accuracy; inside work possible, bottom cutting practical; full diameter; low skill demand.	Expensive; few bearing choices; total cutter extension required; can mar and chatter work; template essential; similar problems of end-bearing bits; incremental not continuous adjustment; sensitive to edge defects.
Edge Guide Easy on router; no defect transfer; lots of nonbearing cutter choices; continuous adjustability; can do router table cuts.	Expensive; not easy to adjust; takes medium to high skill; very sensitive to handling on inside cuts.
Subbase Cheap; fast; simple; can be used where no other system works; can be used with any cutter.	Inaccurate; sensitive to handling on inside cuts; eccentric; usually unstable.
Shank of Tool Accurate; simplest option available; can access tight turns; little or no cutter offset; concentric.	Rare; hard on template; takes medium skill; few cutters will work.
Circle Cutter/Ellipse Maker Very accurate; short learning curve; quality cut; unique to router.	Can be expensive; sliding arm needed for accurate diameters.

Bearing-Guided Cutters

Let's begin with the simplest guide systems—the integral pilots and ball bearings on the bits themselves. Before the ball bearing became popular, the end of the tool bit was ground into a fixed pilot shaft. This pilot will skid (and often smoke) along the work and limits the cutter to the single designed profile. Without the pilot, the cutter will cut willy-nilly into the work. This is an old design, but still can be found on consumer-grade cutters today. The solid pilot is found on a few solid carbide tool bits but is more typical on short-run high-speed steel (HSS) bits. The problem is that router bits turn so fast (20,000 rpm or so) that the fixed pilot shaft can score or, even worse, burn the wood. Today, a ball bearing generally replaces the fixed steel pilot.

A consumer-grade high-speed steel utility bit like the ogee is guided off the steel pilot on its end. This inexpensive tool is for short-run use only.

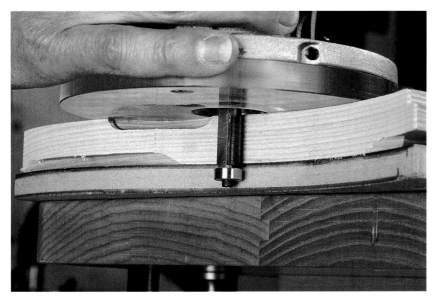

Some of the end-bearing cutters can be used with templates that are placed under the work.

All sorts of router bits use ball bearings on the end. Many are decorative profile cutters, but a few are used to join window sash, make rabbets, slot, or flush trim. They are easy to use and won't burn the stock. Most often they are used for routing on edges and end-grain, or with a template.

It doesn't take much skill to rout with a bearing-guided cutter: You set the depth of cut, lock the motor height and pull the router inboard to get the bearing to engage the work. These cutters are essentially used on the edge of stock, so they are most frequently used in the fixed-base router. Fixed-base routers are more stable than plunge routers and easier to control along the edge.

Ball-bearing cutters solve a lot of problems but they do have a few disadvantages. One is safety. In a roundabout way they force the cutter designer to make larger diameter tools. And big cutters present more risk, not only because they expose more tool, but shift too much of the router off the work. How's that? Well, if a router bit has a $\frac{1}{2}$-in.-diameter bearing on it, it can be as much as $\frac{1}{2}$ in. larger in diameter than it need be if it did not have the bearing. Bearing-guided cutters are used on the edge of the

An offset subbase, at right, substantially increases the stability of the router on corners.

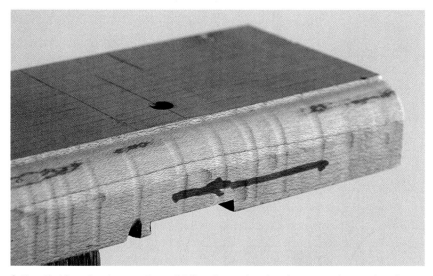

Cutters that have bearings on the end follow the work rather than a template, and tend to transfer defects onto the workpiece.

work, so at no time is a router base sitting on 50 percent of its footprint; 40 percent is more typical, with less than 25 percent at the ends of the cut. Any cutter must reach maximum speed before it touches the stock, so during part of the cut the base casting is shifted even more off the work. For a $1\frac{1}{2}$-in.-diameter cutter in a router with a 6-in.-diameter casting, there is only 37 percent of the footprint on the work on startup, and that isn't a lot of stability.

A bearing-guided cutter simplifies the routing process, eliminates the need for more complicated guide systems, including the router table, and provides the chance to work on assemblies that might otherwise not be routable, such as installed handrails or countertops.

On the downside, bearings follow edge defects. A chattered or rough edge will yield a chattered profile. Bearings, when placed on the end, effectively lengthen the tool bit and the more distant the bearing is from

The side pressure from a bearing can be so high that it mars the work. If this is a problem, sometimes two bearings can be used.

the collet, the more likelihood for chatter, vibration, and wear. Edge- or collar-guided cuts are usually somewhat cleaner than the equivalent bearing-guided. This is a minor disadvantage, but a real one nonetheless.

You also have to consider expense when choosing a bearing-guided cutter. An R-3 ($\frac{3}{16}$-in. bore x $\frac{1}{2}$-in. diameter) is $1 to $3, and frankly, there is little you can do to increase its life. Moreover, small router bearings are made in such volume with lax offshore quality control that high-quality bearing makers in Europe and North America refuse to compete. Consequently, the small router-bit bearings will continue to deteriorate in quality for a while.

Router bit bearings endure the most severe of service conditions. They accelerate from zero to 20,000 rpm in a second or so and decelerate just as fast when in contact with the work. They can't contain much lubrication, so they wear out pretty quickly. A template collar will last for decades; a router-bit bearing can wear out in an hour or two of cumulative use.

A bearing, unlike the other guide systems, will emboss the workpiece. The pressure on this small area is so high that the bearings can easily mar softwoods. Sometimes the design of the cutter will permit two bearings and this may eliminate or reduce the problem.

SHANK BEARING-GUIDED CUTTERS

The cutters with bearings on the shank are designed to work with a template and are often called pattern bits when sold as straight cutters. Since the cutter and bearing are virtually the same diameter, the templates are made to the exact profile of the intended cut. (Note that the collar-guide systems below are more complex to use because of the different diameters and the need to design that into the template.)

The template is one of the keys to unlocking the power of the router. Most cutters will accept bearings on their shanks and it's a good idea to use this combination.

There are a number of cutters usually sold without a top bearing that can easily be fitted with one. These include the dovetail, straight, round-nose, and glue-joint, as well as most small-diameter profile bits. The typical standard bearing dimensions for $\frac{1}{4}$-in, $\frac{3}{8}$-in., and $\frac{1}{2}$-in. shanks are shown in the chart and most are under $10.

By far, the most popular tools with top-mounted bearings are straight bits. These are very accurate, cutting precisely as measured. For example, a straight bit with a diameter of 0.740 in. and bearing outside diameter (OD) of 0.750 in. will cut to within 0.005 in. of the template, always. (Calculation: offset equals bearing diameter minus cutter diameter divided by 2.) For very precise and accurate full or fractional-thickness template cuts, there is no better hand-router guide system. Primary uses are in trimming the workpiece to match the shape of the template, making templates, and joinery.

Standard Bearing and Shank Sizes

THE FIRST NUMBER IN EACH CHART entry, is the bore (the hole) of the bearing. The second number is the diameter. The width (thickness) of the bearings varies, but they are constant within a size; their numbers are not particularly important. Bearing bores can be diminished, within limits, with small precision pressed-on rings. This is a precise machine shop practice and must be done with care. Errors in balance, or a ring that slips off can be hazardous.

Bearings are ground to very tight tolerances. The hardware and cutter geometry for end-of-cutter bearings is such that they should always fit. On occasion they may be difficult to slide onto the shank, however, and may require a press fit. If a shank is too small, leaving some play of the bearing on the shaft, the situation is hazardous and the bearing should not be used. A bearing should have some resistance to its fit on the shank and should be fixed with a shank collar.

STANDARD BEARING AND SHANK SIZES

*Dimensions provided are inside bore first,
followed by the outside diameter.*

End-Mounted Bearings	Shank-Mounted Bearings
⅛ in. x ⅜ in.	¼ in. x ½ in.
³⁄₁₆ in. x ⅜ in.	¼ in. x ⅝ in.
³⁄₁₆ in. x ½ in.	¼ in. x ¾ in.
	⅜ in. x ⅞ in.
	⅜ in. x 1⅛ in.
	½ in. x ¾ in.
	½ in. x 1⅛ in.
	½ in. x 1⅜ in.

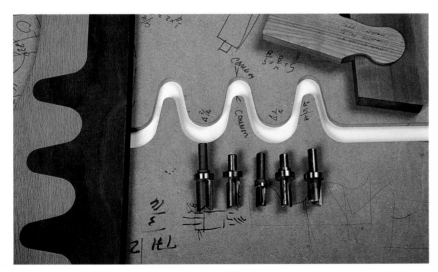

A router with pattern bits and a template can handle curved joinery with tight turns.

Problems do exist with matching the shank, flute lengths and such with the thickness of the template and work. Since the whole flute has to be extended for the bearing to engage the template, it is possible that a mismatch will occur (a long fluted cutter and a skinny workpiece, for

One manufacturer, PRC, has designed a set of pattern bits for templates up to ¾ in. thick and material up to 1½ in. Two of the cutters are offset to pretrim the work to ¹⁄₁₆ in. proud of the template.

Cutting a simple dado is one of the most straightforward jobs for a router. Here the author is using a pattern bit, with the bearing mounted on the top, that follows a straightedge placed on the cut line.

The bearing-guided straight bit will produce a copy of the template profile.

example.) Too much cutter extension is always hazardous. In response to this dilemma, PRC (see sources) has designed a set of cutters for any practical thickness of template (¼ to ¾ in.) and workpiece thickness to 1½ in. The system uses five cutters, two of which have a ¹⁄₁₆-in. offset built into them so the final pass with the flush trimmers will be smoother, with a constant ¹⁄₁₆-in. overhang.

The negatives of the end-bearing bits also apply to the top-bearing bits, but a little less so. (They still have relatively short lives and transmit template edge defects and wear on the router.) On the other hand, the bearings are right up against the collet, so there is less stress; also, bearings for shanks are bigger, hold more lube and last longer.

Two other positive points with these cutters include their access to the work and their ability to bottom cut more than their diameter. A template can be placed anywhere on the work, which means that edge, end, inside blind, through, and half-blind cuts are possible with these cutters. Also, because the bottom of these tools are ground to bottom cut, they can excavate an area greater than their diameter.

Collar Guides

Template collar guides, like pattern bits, are essentially used only with templates. They behave similarly to pattern bits as they surround the router bit just like a bearing. There are four similar types of collar systems.

Collar guides are used with templates for joinery, like cutting this half lap.

The collar guide and cutter essentially act like a pattern bit with a bearing on top, shown at left.

Porter-Cable, the oldest and most popular, has a two-piece ring and nut assembly that fastens to the subbase. Bosch has a bayonet fastening system (like the lenses of some cameras in which you insert the collar that locks into place) that fastens to an accessory that is screwed to the subbase. Milwaukee has a collar that's screwed directly to the plastic subbase. And there are others that fasten to the base casting. (Almost all router manufacturers make accessories for the Porter-Cable system as well as their own.)

Collars come in a variety of diameters and lengths, sometimes for very specific jobs.

The length of the collar should wind up just shy of the thickness of your thinnest template. I use ⅜-in. or thicker templates, so I've hacksawn my collars to ⁵⁄₁₆ in.

The Porter-Cable collar guide system, here on its 42193 offset router base, provides a simple way to use a variety of bushing sizes on the same router. They are interchangeable and fit in the ring assembly.

Three of the most common collar-guide systems: (left to right) Bosch, Porter-Cable, and Milwaukee.

A collar-guide system cuts a path that's offset from the bushing—so you need to take that into account when designing templates.

Double Duty from Collars

Router-bit guide collars are so cheap I usually buy them in pairs. With the same diameter collar in two different routers you can do both rough and finish work with the same setup. With two different diameter cutters, you can let the first router do the dirty work and let the second router, with a slightly bigger cutter and set slightly deeper, clean up and finish the job. This way, they last longer so you can get more mileage out of them.

One disadvantage to the collar system is that the collar is always larger than the cutter it surrounds. This means that the template cut is magnified on outside radii and smaller with concave curves. This discrepancy is calculated by subtracting the radius of the collar from the radius of the bit. Make your template smaller or larger to account for this difference.

Collar use is never as precise and predictable as bearing-guided cutters. A collar must be within 0.001 in. of center or so for it to be practically concentric to the cutter. This rarely happens, and it is not uncommon for a cutter to be off from center by $\frac{1}{16}$ in. or more. The Bosch self-centering collar system is said to be adjustable to within 0.004 in. of center. To minimize the error caused by the eccentricity, don't rotate the router as you guide it against the template. Keep the handles, for example, in the same orientation to the work as you move the router in the cut.

The collar has a special safety advantage in that you can always extend just the right amount of cutter for the job. Any excessive cutter beyond the subbase should be minimized. For full thickness cuts, project the bit $\frac{1}{16}$ in. beyond the material thickness.

On the down side, the maximum extension of any cutter is compromised by the use of collars; almost all of the collet nuts on all routers will hit some part of the collar. If the collar is not used, the cutter may be extended further. Cutter extension and length, template, subbase and workpiece thickness are always in conflict with bearings and collars. As a rule, the practical and safe limit for full-thickness cuts with bearing-guided router cutters is 2 in. but $1\frac{1}{2}$ in. when collars are used. Thicker stock can be routed, but probably should be worked on a shaper. Cutters larger than $1\frac{1}{8}$ in. will not enter the bore of most collars.

Also, collar guides, like edge guides and pattern bits, will allow the cutter to transfer template defects to the work.

Edge Guides

These accessories use a pair of rods that fit into the router's base casting, providing a way to fasten a small fence that guides the router parallel to the workpiece edge. The advantages include continuous adjustability and the larger contact surface, which tends to even out minor imperfections in the edge and provide a smoother cut.

Edge guides do limit the travel of the router to a line parallel to the edge of the work, whether curved or straight. They consist of three components: the pair of rods, a body, and a fence. The fence can be straight or radiused to match curved work. Each guide is designed expressly for its router, though an aftermarket version, the Micro Fence, is available to fit all popular routers. Typical cuts are along the edge, across the ends, or across the width of stock. Edge guides don't have the work access of a collar guide and template and they are sensitive to workpiece size. For example, narrow stock, less than the radius of the base casting, does not present enough surface for the stability of the router.

Edge guides are relatively inexpensive, don't mar the work and are continuously adjustable because the body/fence can be positioned anywhere along the rods. This flexibility is precisely what makes them useful, especially for the shop-made mortiser. Oddly, I find they work poorly on most other jigs. They are usually used directly on the work.

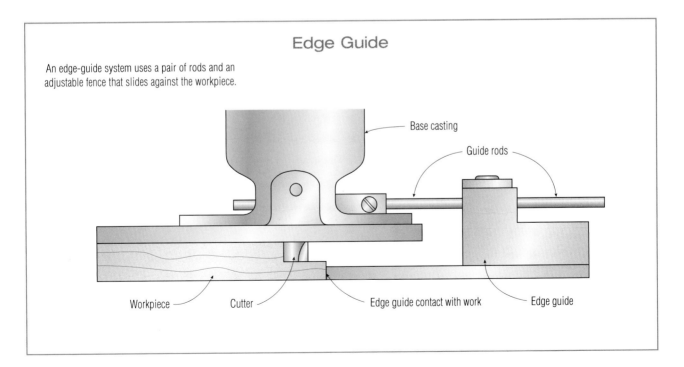

Edge Guide

An edge-guide system uses a pair of rods and an adjustable fence that slides against the workpiece.

Base casting

Guide rods

Workpiece — Cutter — Edge guide contact with work — Edge guide

This homemade edge guide is made from hardwood, aluminum bar and steel rod.

This aftermarket edge guide from Micro Fence uses a micrometer-style adjustment for precision.

Edge guides can be easily adjusted to vary the width of a cut. A ½-in. bit, for example, can make a ⅝-in.-wide rabbet.

Since edge guides correspond to the fence on the router table, they can be used, at times, in the absence of one, but never as a substitute. With simple, small-diameter cutters you can make raised panels, for instance. This is messy, but the cutters are small and thus safe to use in this way.

Edge guides are clumsy; don't expect to work one of these perfectly on your first try. Note that the end of a cutting pass can be a problem because only half of the fence remains in contact as you finish the cut. Unless you practice keeping that small portion in contact with the workpiece, the router will pivot and spoil the cut. There are three simultaneous functions for you to control: hold-in, hold-down, and slide-along. On an inside cut, any deviation of the fence from the edge of the work will ruin the cut. On an edge cut, you just recut without a penalty if the fence strays from the

The author's mortising jig employs edge guides and stops to confine the cutter pathway to a square or rectangular hole.

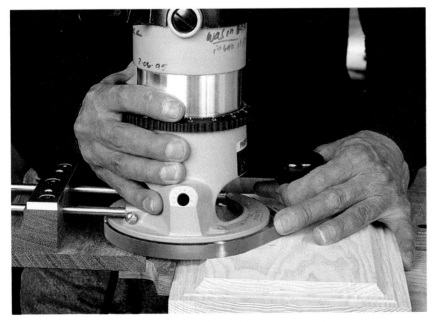

Keeping the whole setup flat is important when making a raised panel.

Offset Subbase for Added Stability

All routers are unstable when half or less of the base casting is on the work. An offset rectangular subbase can overcome instability and, when used with a straightedge, provide a secure and accurate guide mechanism. With one side of the subbase longer than the other, it's much easier to apply pressure over the workpiece and keep the router from tipping.

A square subbase provides a very accurate guide surface. If you work the same edge of the base against the template and locate the template in the same place, all similar cuts will be the same.

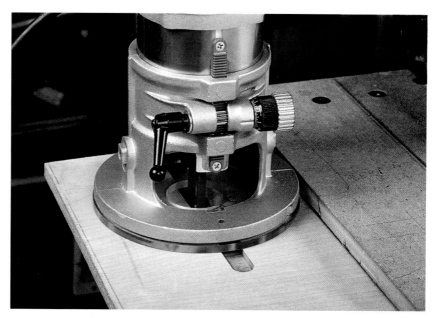

A round subbase is not a precise guide for routing. Any rotation of subbase can cause a widening of the dado because cutters are rarely perfectly centered.

workpiece. An offset subbase, such as the Porter-Cable 42193, can consolidate the handling functions and shorten your learning curve.

The Subbase

The subbase itself can be used as a router guide with a curved template or straightedge. It is the least accurate but quickest to set up. You clamp a stick down on the work, hold the router against it and rout; it's fast but never predictable or precise. Cutters are never well-centered to the diameter of a round subbase, so any rotation of the router during the cut will be expressed in a less-than-perfect cut. (Plunge router base castings come in many shapes—consequently the edge can't be used as a guide to find the center.)

The problem of guiding directly off the router base isn't limited to the "center anomaly," however. Routing directly on the work against a clamped-down straightedge will cause the router to deviate as chip flotsam bounces and collects between router and the guide. Moreover, the surface tearout and chip accumulation under the router will interfere with its travel and result in variations of cutting depth. Clearly, routing with the base casting or subbase as a guide should be a last resort—not a first approach.

An advantage to using the router base as a guide is that you can use any cutter and to its maximum depth. There are no bearings to engage or collars to frustrate the reach of the cutter. I discovered this by accident while trying to make a long tenon cut with a short cutter and collar with a template. The square-edge subbase guaranteed a straight cut at a constant depth, and let me extend the short cutter to its maximum depth for the length of tenon I needed.

Tool Shank

Like the fixed-pilot shaft on the end of the tool, the shank of the tool can also be used as a guide, but only for short durations with small-diameter bits. You should never use the shank as a guide if the tool's cutting diameter is greater than the shank. This is strictly a small, straight tool proposition, and a template of some sort is essential.

You can use a ¼-in. straight bit, for example, from the inside of a series of drawer openings covered with plastic laminate. You'll punch through the plastic laminate and then allow the shank of the bit to ride against the solid wood that essentially forms the pattern, which amounts to two operations at once (the cutout and the flush trim). Once in a blue moon, I may use the shank of the tool when making complementary templates from a master to minimize the offset. I have also used the shanks of short, ¼-in. solid carbide straight bits to get into tight corners of template mortises. In any event, the shanks get hot and the template (unless of plastic laminate)

Just as the end of the tool can be used as a guide, so can its shank. The cutting diameter of the tool must be equal to or less than the shank diameter. This practice should be confined to small (less than ½ in.) diameter straight bits and limited to very short duty.

Compare the radii of the corners of these mortises. Obviously, the small cutter cuts a nearly square corner.

gets worn quickly, so this is more of a curiosity than a viable and important method of router pathway control.

The Circle Cutter

A router fastened to a stick with an adjustable arm, or with just a hole in it for a pivot, can cut the circumference of a circle. This is an interesting method of pathway control. The router has nowhere to go but in a circle, and the cuttings are excellent. You will need a small plunge router to do this safely. It is messy, as this is a full-diameter cutter pathway, but there are several plunge routers with vacuum attachments that will collect the chips.

It is interesting that there are so few low-tech, low-skill processes in routing that are so precise and easy. There are ellipse makers that work well also, but aside from circles, segments of circles, and ellipses, I don't know of any other uses of a router tethered to a point or points. It seems there should be more here. Without much ado, I can make a circle within 0.001 in. of its intended diameter with a $100 plunge router, a $10 bit, a dollar's worth of medium density fiberboard, and a pivot stick, all in just a few minutes.

The author's circle cutter confines the cutter pathway to one fixed radius.

This slot-making jig limits the slot length with a stop. The slot width is one cutter diameter because the collar can't squiggle in its slot.

Other Guide Options

Usually one guide system per operation is all that is necessary. For example, a collar guide is usually not required when a bearing-guided cutter is in play, but it can be. I use subbase stops and edge guides to control the cutter pathway when making mortises, and I also use a subbase stop and collar guide with my slot maker to define the length of the slots it makes. The point is that there are multiple options for all your needs.

Freehand unguided routing is artwork You can learn to carve and waste freehand, but it will take time. Small, light routers with lots of cutter visibility (PC 100, DeWalt 610) will give you the best chance. If sign-making is your thing, work with big letters at shallow depths. Sharp cutters are essential. High-speed steel can be ground to a sharper edge than carbide; it may be the better choice if you have the grinding skills to keep it sharp.

Templates Go First

When making disks or rings, having a template at hand removes virtually all the risk. The procedure is to make the template (⅜-in. or ½-in. medium-density fiberboard) trace its circumference on the work, bandsaw the disk leaving ⅛ in. outside the line, clamp the template to the work and rout to pattern with a pattern bit. There is no need to poke a hole in the work for the pivot.

Fixed-Base Routers

I n the United States, the fixed-base router has been the dominant router design for over half a century. The tool is simple, with few moving parts, and in my view is safer than a plunge router for most operations. The motor, clamped firmly (fixed) in its base casting, has a simple depth adjustment, but it must be stopped and reset between cuts. The plunge router overcomes this disadvantage, and is the tool of choice for deep mortises that must be cut in several passes (see chapter 4).

This 1960s-vintage Black & Decker model 442 is still running.

A fixed-base router, left, is best applied in single-depth edge cuttings. The plunge router, right, is designed for successive depth changes under power and is best for multistage inside excavations like mortises.

Fixed-Base Router

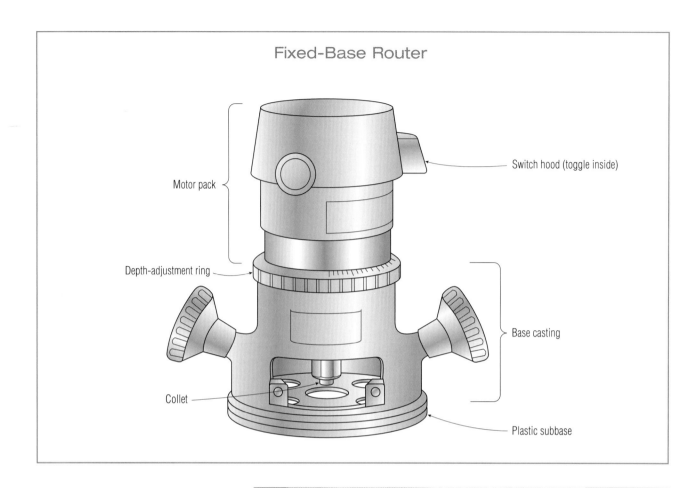

Motor pack

Switch hood (toggle inside)

Depth-adjustment ring

Base casting

Collet

Plastic subbase

Cross grain dadoes and dovetails are easily cut with a fixed-base router and collar guide.

The plunge router allows you to change its cutter depth because a trigger or latch releases the locking mechanism to lower the cutter into the workpiece with the base fully supported. This is risky if these same maneuvers are tried with the fixed-base tool: Because it must be tipped, the base won't be fully supported as the cutter enters the work. But the additional weight and overall awkwardness of the plunge router make it unsuitable for a lot of the general routing we do along edges and against templates.

Router Basics

The anatomy of the fixed-base router is quite simple and has remained essentially the same since it first came on the scene. The motor is packaged in a precision-ground cylinder that fits precisely in a matching aluminum base casting. All of the motors have bearings on either end of their armatures, a pair of carbon brushes that transmit electrical current to the armature, and a collet (see the sidebar below) fixed to the business end of the tool. The positioning of the motors in the base castings varies from manufacturer to manufacturer, as well as the knob assemblies, castings, switches, wire sets, and collets.

Router Collets

ALL COLLETS MADE TODAY are multislotted except the short ones in trimmers, and the fixed-base DeWalt 610. They are connected to their collet nuts and as such pull themselves out of the router when unwound from the armature. Cutters sticking in the router are a thing of the past.

There is still a lot of design variation, however. The slotting varies. The slots originate from one or both ends of the collet. Some have three, six, or eight slots. The components vary in length, wall thickness, and materials—though all are steel. The nuts can be square, hexagonal, or octagonal. One thing is constant: They all hold the cutter and hold it well if you apply 15 or so pounds of squeeze to a 10-in. set of wrenches.

Use no abrasives to keep them clean. They are made to very tight tolerances. Clean the dust out of them and the collet seat if they get dirty. If a cutter slips in a collet, you should probably scrap it, especially if it is scratched or burred. Worn collets don't hold the cutter well and out-of-balance tool bits will vibrate more in a worn collet. Keep at least ¾ in. of shank in the collet and whenever possible use the

entire length of the collet for maximum holding power. Do not use any of the shank in the collet where the flute fades away from grinding, because the holding power will be compromised.

Knocking Off the Sharp Edges

Base and motor castings can be a bit rough, and sharp enough in some places to cut you. An accidental quick grab for a cutter change, storage, installation of a guide collar, or router control can result in injury. I spend 10 minutes with a deburring tool on any new casting. You can also use a file and a wire brush.

Many router castings can use some deburring to get rid of jagged edges. A deburring tool like this one is a $10 purchase.

The underside of motor caps can be sharp. I dropped this router, saving it from a crash, but then cut myself on the cap reaching for it.

CASTINGS, HANDLES, AND SWITCHES

Base castings vary and are quite distinguishable. All have windows for good cutter visibility, though most base plates are black and hide the work surface. DeWalt and Porter-Cable will supply accessory transparent subbase replacements. A router that can readily stand upside down for bit changes is a nice convenience. Porter-Cable, DeWalt, and Milwaukee have accounted for this. The Bosch model has a radius on the motor cap for comfort, but at some expense for upside down stability.

The knob or handle assemblies of most fixed-base routers are placed low on the machine and provide stability. Plastic, wood, and metal are the typical materials, and most people will have their own opinions on which are most comfortable. I use an offset subbase on all of my fixed-base routers, and I control the tool with one hand on the base casting and the other on the offset base. This configuration allows maximum control especially around the corners and along the edges of the work. However, you should be aware that the position of the two casting knobs supplied with a router is well thought out. So give them a good try before considering any changes.

Wire sets are either two- or three-conductor depending on how the tool is insulated. Double-insulated tools will have two-prong plugs without the ground. All commercial routers use rubber jacketed wire sets but most are different lengths. I am 6 ft. tall and I always use an extension cord, but I would like the plug to remain on the ground and for me that means a 10-ft. wire set.

The DeWalt 610 shown here can be supplied with a clear plastic, round replacement subbase for collar guide use. The flat head provides a stable base for turning it upside down for bit changes.

The maple knobs on the Bosch subbase get you as close to the work as any router.

The Porter-Cable model 690 base casting is the perfect size for my hand. I've got the same control on this router as the quarterback has on the football.

Switches are slide, toggle, rocker or trigger, and their locations vary. I would not select a router based on the switch; it's a good idea to clarify the off position so you know the tool is off when you plug it in 10 ft. away. Also, prepare yourself for a quick stop and keep your hands in a conven-

For added safety, the author highlights the off direction on the switch.

ient location for hitting the off button easily. You never know when a clamp may slip or something else go awry.

POWER

Fixed-base routers in the commercial class range from about 1 to 3 hp. Weight and appropriate applications scale up with the power; expect about 7 or 8 pounds difference within this power range. More power also means more metal and consequently the capacity to soak up heat. A router in heavy use can heat up, and if the heat exceeds the cooling fan's capacity, then the router gets hot to the touch. However, the longer it takes to heat up, the less likely it will break down from overload. So if your router is consistently hot, reduce the load or get a bigger router.

Porter-Cable has every power range covered—from ⅞ hp to 3¼ hp. DeWalt's only entry is 1.5 hp; Bosch has models in 1¾ hp and 2 hp; and Milwaukee in 1½ hp and 2 hp Ryobi, Makita, and Sears/Craftsman also have fixed-base entrants of various strengths, but Makita is the only commercial-grade tool with two entries at 1 hp and 1⅜ hp. Porter-Cable has an exclusive in the sustained all-day power class (7518), and there are no other fixed-base routers of its size (3 hp).

D-HANDLED ROUTERS

The D-handled router is the least popular fixed-base design and the most costly. It does enjoy a limited niche market, however. Its advocates claim safety and control because a pistol-style switch is gripped to start the router. To stop, you just release. With the switch in hand, you can shut down quickly, but in my view that safety margin is more than offset by a loss of control. A D-handled router is always held the same way and has less stability as you finish a pass at the end of the workpiece. Moreover, the obligatory D-handle in line with the travel of the router interferes with cuts made with edge guides and collar guides.

The D-handled style of router provides one-handed control, which is often convenient for repetitive work.

The Porter-Cable 691 D-handle casting.

The Industry Standard

THE PORTER-CABLE 690 IS THE most popular commercial-grade medium weight fixed-base router in North America. The motor is trapped in its base casting with four pins, which allows it to turn and move easily up and down when you release the clamp. It's a simple but effective method of raising and lowering the cutter.

One side of the base casting has been actually sawn in half so the motor clamp will evenly squeeze down on the motor for a firm grip. However, for me, its base-tightening thumbscrew is too small, and I have replaced mine with a lever. The motor travel in its base is about 1¾ in. with all four pins engaged. (It is not advisable to operate the tool without all of its pins engaged in the base casting.)

Porter-Cable 690

This 8-lb., 1.5-hp, single-speed, hard-start router has the smallest base casting in its class. But the weight and balance of the 690 is about right for most cutters less than 1⅝ in. long and 1⅝ in. diameter. The 690 sits easily upside down on its flat motor cap for bit changes. Two wrenches of the same size are required to change cutters. Its collet design is self-releasing and very effective. There are six sizes: ¼ in., ⅜ in., ½ in., 8mm, 10mm, and 12mm.

The Porter-Cable enjoys popularity like no other router. Many accessories, jigs and fixtures are designed around the 690. It has a low center of gravity and is comfortable to use. The 690 applies itself best to fixed-depth edge and template cuts. I would not have the 690 serve as the only router in a shop, but I would consider it as a first purchase. As a bonus, its base casting also accepts the smaller ⅞-hp motor for light work.

Porter-Cable 690	
Weight	8 lbs.
Speed	Single, 23,000 rpm
Amps	10
Soft start	no
Horsepower	1.5
Height adjuster/mechanism	Continuous, motor twist
Collets	¼ in., ½ in., ⅜ in., & metrics option
Baseplate diameter	5¾ in.

The squat casting, shown with upgraded lock lever and accessory offset base provides so much control that it can feel like an extension of your hands.

Leading Fixed-Base Routers

There is no single perfect router. Most have some excellent features, but make compromises in other important areas. Some are old designs that still work well; others offer new solutions to some sticky problems. The DeWalt 610, for example, is a quality tool that's been in production virtually unchanged for over 30 years (first as a Black & Decker tool and Elu tool). On the other hand, the Bosch 1617EVS is a relatively new tool with some innovative features. Each of the routers has its own personality and its own set of strengths and weaknesses.

THE DEWALT 610

As mentioned above, the DeWalt 610 design is at least 30 years old and essentially unchanged. A rack and pinion gear raises and lowers the motor in the housing. It can be adjusted, like the 690, to zero at any point in its

DeWalt 610	
Weight	7.3 lbs.
Speed	Single, 25,000 rpm
Amp	9
Soft start	no
Horsepower	1.5
Height adjuster/mechanism	Rack & pinion
Collets	¼ in. & ½ in.
Baseplate diameter	6 in. (shown with an accessory offset base)

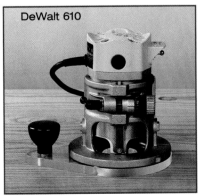

DeWalt 610

The three motor pack projections add another 1 in. of travel to this DeWalt 610, which is also shown with round collet nut and collar.

travel and its depth ring is indicated in ¹⁄₆₄ths. A wing nut is standard for tightening the casting around the motor, but a short lever is better (a Reid tool, KHB-14, for example). The casting is not sawn through as on Porter-Cable; rather, a ¾-in. strap (band) of the casting is cinched on the motor on the rack side of the base. The grip is not as sure compared with the Porter-Cable, but the motor never slips.

Two positive changes in the DeWalt 610 that warrant praise are its collet nut and motor barrel extensions. The collet nut has been milled to fit inside its accessory collar guides. The closer the collet can get to its template, the less deflection there is with the cutter—a nice touch. The 610 (and its ancestors) have never had much up and down motor travel and used to be quite popular in the router table nevertheless. When the tool carried the Elu and Black & Decker labels, its motor pack was redesigned to accept a longer rack for its depth pinion gear. This clever change added another ⅞ in. of travel for a total of about 1¾ in. However, more travel is at the expense of security. If the 1¾-in. depth is exceeded, the base casting's grip on the motor pack isn't secure.

The 610 hard-start, 1½-hp router is more sensitive to cutter imbalance than other routers its size. It's fine with small, squatty profile cutters like ogees, roundovers and bevels, but it vibrates more than I like with long (1½ in.) cutters of equivalent diameter. This gets more pronounced with bearing-guided router bits. The motor rests well upside down for cutter changes, and requires two different size wrenches to unlock its collet. Through the succeeding years its castings have deteriorated some and self-tapping subbase screws have replaced through-hole machine tapping.

While under the Elu label, the 610's collet was at its best: eight-slotted and self-releasing. Under the DeWalt label the collet was simplified to a single slit, nonreleasing design. Its short length (¾ in.) probably contributes to its vibration sensitivity. Nevertheless, it does grip the cutter well and cutters do not stick in the collet.

The 610 accepts few accessories, but DeWalt does have clear round and offset subbases for this tool in their catalog. With its short, stable geometry, its ability to project the collet into a collar guide, and with its transparent accessory subbase, the tool is particularly well suited for dovetail and box-joint template work. It is just as stable along the edge of stock with decorator cutters. The early Black & Decker tools with essentially the same design were designed to go right back to work after a 6-ft. drop to the floor. The switches last forever but the wire sets seem to have about a two-year life span if used regularly.

THE BOSCH 1617EVS

Bosch is the first to produce an all-new router since the Porter-Cable 690 crossed over from Rockwell. It is, however, a standard-looking router and requires close inspection and a few practice cuts to be appreciated.

The base casting is equipped with a two-stage depth adjuster. It is by no means a micrometer, but small, continuous depth changes can be made by turning the screw adjuster while the motor lock is disengaged. The motor has three small rectangular notches on ½-in. centers milled into it or on opposite sides. The depth adjuster engages a notch for its rough position and the vernier is used for the fine adjust. The total motor travel is about 1¹¹⁄₁₆ in. It's not a good idea to exceed that. If the motor isn't engaged with its depth adjuster assembly, the lock system won't work properly. One interesting note: The motor can be inserted in two diametrically opposed positions within the casting, so that you can easily adjust the switch position for ease of operation.

BOSCH 1617EVS

Bosch 1617EVS	
Weight	7.7 lbs.
Speed	Variable, 8,000–25,000 rpm
Amps	12
Soft start	Yes
Horsepower	2
Height adjuster/mechanism	Three ½-in. increments, with secondary continuous micro
Collets	¼ in., ½ in., & ⅜ in.
Baseplate diameter	6 in.

A spring lock engages a notch in the casting for the rough ½-in. changes on the Bosch 1617.

Bosch designed this tool with variable speed, double insulation and soft start. The castings are magnesium, and with its 2-hp motor it's as light as the DeWalt 610. High power and light weight don't usually go together. You might expect the tool to run away from you like its 1604 single speed predecessor. On the contrary, the 1617EVS is a delight to rout with.

The collet seat is milled right into the end of the armature; there are no couplings. This, along with its precision bearings, alignment, armature design, and balance make this the smoothest-running motor of all the routers I know of.

Bosch has solved the motor lock problem that plagues some other routers. The base casting is split through its height on one side and has a very user-friendly over-center lever lock much like a toggle clamp. It is adjustable for wear and stretch, and is designed for a close fit between the motor and the base casting.

The base casting is drilled for its own subbase, and has the same three-hole pattern used for the Porter-Cable 690 specialty accessory subbases and router table. The design of the interior of the base casting and its subbase allows the guide collar to get within 0.004 in. or better of center. The 1617EVS is useful for all fixed-depth cutting with a 2-hp router. It has unique advantages in close quarters, and its forgiving soft start will prevent an unwanted kick into an uncut area. Moreover, its feedback electronics start the tool gradually (soft start) and provide a new measure of safety not found in hard-start tools. The 1617EVS can also absorb kinetic accidents such as an unexpected dig into the uncut material. If I'm into experimental work, I'll choose the 1617EVS for this reason, because routing can be dicey. In ordinary work, the motor behaves like a single-speed tool, but if there is an instantaneous overload this is the router I want to be using. It also has an additional ¼-hp rating over the single-speed 1617 for this purpose.

MILWAUKEE 5680

The Milwaukee is a 2 hp, single-speed hard-start commercial grade router that has remained essentially unchanged for its lifetime of over 20 years.

The motor height is adjusted with a plastic ring engaged in a spiral ground around the outside of the motor. The motor is "hung" in the casting by this ring, so the mechanism doesn't work when the router is upside down. It's not a great choice for the router table. There's also no way to "zero" the vertical position in the router. All depth changes are therefore relative to the last reading of the depth ring. The motor travel is about 1½ in.; after that, the casting begins to lose its grip on the motor.

Milwaukee is credited with the first multisplit self-releasing collet. Its 1⅛-in. overall length and eight-sided nut is a combination not to be found in any other router. The motor has a very flat and large head for easy bit changes upside down.

The Milwaukee 5680 is one of the noisiest and toughest of routers, designed to flop around in the back of a pickup truck, and has long been the standard for carpenters and outside tradesmen. The 5680 is well balanced and ergonomically acceptable, but the initial kick-back on startup has got to be the most powerful of any 2-hp tool. Its squat, heavy motor helps keep the tool flat on edge cuts.

Prevent Accidental Gouging

A powerful router, especially one without a soft-start feature, will lurch when you first flip the switch. To help prevent contact with the workpiece, keep the router a full router-bit diameter away from the work at startup.

Milwaukee 5680	
Weight	8.5 lbs.
Speed	Single, 26,000 rpm
Amps	12
Soft start	no
Horsepower	2
Height adjuster/mechanism	Ring-hung motor, twist ring
Collets	¼ in., ½ in., & ⅜ in.
Baseplate diameter	6 in. (shown with an accessory offset base)

Milwaukee 5680

The Milwaukee 5680 has the only eight-sided collet nut and is one of the first with an eight-slotted self-releasing collet.

The Milwaukee castings are better than most, but still need some deburring. In my view, their split-base casting design holds the motor well but their wing nut assembly for tightening is too small. I've replaced mine with a set screw and nut. The unique screw-on collar guide system, ample motor travel, and high power of this router make it particularly useful for dovetail/box joint template work, all edge cuttings, and pattern cuts.

THE PORTER-CABLE 7518

The Porter-Cable 7518 is the largest fixed-base router. Bosch and Black & Decker used to compete in this niche but the 7518 is now alone in this class. It's not often this happens. I suspect the reason for this is pricing and the economies of scale; nevertheless, this is just a lot of router at a price

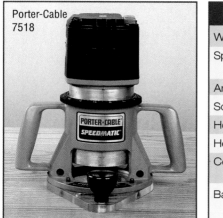

Porter-Cable 7518

Porter-Cable 7518	
Weight	14.5 lbs.
Speed:	Variable, 5 speed 10,000–21,000 rpm
Amps	15
Soft start	Yes
Horsepower	3.25
Height adjuster/mechanism	Continuous motor twist
Collets	¼ in., ½ in., ⅜ in., & metrics option
Baseplate diameter	7 in. (shown with accessory offset base)

With its long motor barrel the Porter-Cable 7518 has more up and down travel than any router, fixed or plunge.

that can't be beat. This heavy-duty machine is the most powerful fixed-base U.S. router at 110 volts and 3¼ hp. Everything about this router is big. It weighs in at more than 1½ times (14.5 lbs.) its closest rival. It has at least as much up-and-down motor travel as any router. It has the largest base casting footprint of any router. And it has an overall height of more than a foot. One would expect this machine to be hard to handle, and it can be with big cutters, but it is deceptively tractable in normal use.

The motor fits in twin spirals within the base casting and one motor revolution translates into 1 in. of cutter height change. The tool is double insulated, soft start, and incrementally variable in steps of 3,000 rpm.

The five-speed motor is very well balanced dynamically and with its massive armature and bearings able to absorb kinetic accidents and tolerate out-of-balance cutters better than most routers regardless of size. If it's power I need, I use the 7518. If a new big cutter is suspicious (perhaps resharpened and out of balance), the 7518 at 10,000 rpm is my proving-ground tool. With its locomotive glide and flywheel momentum, it is a graceful and fun router, whether engaged in light work or heavy lifting.

All Porter-Cable routers use the same two stamped wrenches for their self-releasing collets. The base casting of the 7518 has two cast D-handles and the same small wing nut to tighten its split casting on the motor.

Porter-Cable supplies specialty square, round, and offset subbases, edge guides, collars, and dust collection accessories for their fixed-base routers.

The best use of this router is in heavy fixed-depth long duration cuttings of all sorts, especially deep template cuts for pattern work. The 7518 has the power to break small cutters if overfed, but small cutters should be used in smaller routers. It is also my choice for testing, new, oversize, or prototyped tool bits, jigs and fixtures. If these won't work with the 7518, they won't work with a lesser tool. The tool has become the industry standard for the router table.

MAKITA RF-1101

This 2¼-hp fixed-base router is the newest entry in this category. It has state-of-the-art features such as variable speed, a soft start, and low noise output. It's nicely finished with respectable ergonomics and balance. The tool somewhat resembles both the PC-690 and the Bosch-1617. My sample weighed in at just over 8 lbs., which is similar to other comparable routers.

The over-center toggle motor lock is excellent, but it will pinch you if you're not careful. The wide 4-in.-diameter motor top provides a stable platform so you can easily perform bit changes with the router upside down. Collets are nicely machined and hold cutters well; they use two stamped steel wrenches. The base casting is very similar to the Porter-Cable 609 and accepts Porter-Cable subbases, as well as collar and edge guides.

Makita RF-1101

Makita RF-1101	
Weight	8.06 lbs.
Speed	8,000-24,000 rpm
Amps	11
Soft start	yes
Horsepower	2.25
Collets	¼ in. & ½ in.
Depth adjust mechanism	4 casting pins engage 2 motor pack ground helixes
Baseplate diameter	5¾ in.

The up-and-down motor slop is substantial, and, as such, depth adjustments may take several tries. There is about 1¾ in. of motor travel once all four pins in the base casting engage both ground helixes in the motor pack. The depth adjustment ring is all black, difficult to read with the engraved numbers, and hard to turn. The depth ring can, however, be set to zero at any position, making the setting operation easier. The small toggle switch position changes (with respect to the handle axis) as the motor rotates in the base. It is handy for this woodworker but, at a glance, I can't tell if it's on or off. This is not an exclusive Makita oversight.

Department Store Routers

There are perhaps eight to 12, 1-hp to 2-hp "consumer grade" fixed-base routers on the shelf at any one time. Ryobi and Craftsman are the primary players. Often they are the same tool with different labels. Their prices may vary from $50 to $100. These tools are typically loaded with attractive features but accessories that are often troublesome. In my view, the simplest of these tools is usually the most useful. For occasional light duty weekend hobby work the consumer tool will be acceptable. They are often designed only for ¼-in. shaft bits and should not be expected to compete with industrial/commercial routers.

Sears offers a comprehensive selection of cutters and accessories for their routers. If you are uncertain of your future in woodworking, you can test the waters with a minimum investment with these tools and I'd recommend it. On the other hand, just because a tool, a car, or whatever is relegated to part-time use, that is no excuse for a compromise if a quality product is affordable.

Best Fixed-Base Applications

Fixed-base routers are more stable than plunge routers along the edge of the work—especially with an offset subbase. They are also valuable on inside cuttings if there is a pathway for the cutter from the edge. The blind inside cut with a fixed base is dangerous and requires a plunge router. A bit that's jabbed into an inside excavation will self-feed the router—and you may lose control.

Fixed-base tools, then, because of their low centers, work better on the outside edges of the work or off a template. Your first choice for dovetail, template tools, open dadoes, full or fractional thickness template cuts, and all ball-bearing profile cutters should be the fixed-base router.

Deep cuts are also less risky with a fixed-base router. The levers and knobs of plunge routers are, by design, higher than those of the fixed-base; they are, after all, fastened to the motor head, not the base casting. Deep

Basic notches are another strong point of the fixed-base router.

This step and repeat decorative cove can be managed well with a fixed-base router, a collar guide and an offset subbase. Make sure to pull the collar firmly against the template. Any deviation will spoil the whole pattern.

Fixed-base tools are the best choice for template-edge cuts. They have a low center of gravity and are less likely to tip than a plunge router.

plunge router cuts with a cutter fully extended may cause a router to tip as you push the tool along, especially with a short-base footprint in the direction of travel. (Plunge routers don't generally have round subbases.) All fixed-base routers have round subbases that better support the tool under these conditions.

The fixed-base router is a necessary router for the lifetime woodworker or hobbyist. Neither a plunge nor fixed-base router will cover all types of routing safely—so plan on owning one of each.

Plunge Routers

T he plunge router, which has been around for about 50 years, differs from a fixed-base tool primarily with the integration of the motor with the rest of the tool and the incorporation of a pair of tubes that provide the mechanism for controlling the up-and-down motion. The whole assembly is designed to function as a single unit and doesn't come apart for bit changes or anything else.

All plunge routers all comprised of a base casting, and the two polished tubes for the motor to "pogo" (move up and down) on. A stop turret is a common feature and used to regulate the depth changes. An up-stop is often used to set the motor head at the same starting point. Also standard on most plunge routers are motor locks, handles, switches, edge-guide accessories, depth gauges, and split self-releasing collets. Some other useful features sometimes found are: a soft start so the machine doesn't jump when you flip the switch; variable speed; two-step safety switches; vacuum funnels for chip collection; spindle locks; protective bellows for the plunge tubes; two-stage microadjusters for precise depth control; and electric braking.

Plunge routers are designed to be used in your hands with the aid of gravity; they aren't really meant for the router table where many of them are found today. (The issue of just what makes a good table router will be discussed in chapter 6.) In my view, the plunge router can be utilized wherever use of the fixed-base seems risky or is clumsy. To be sure, a plunge router can be modified, jigged or fixtured for nearly any cut that a fixed-base machine can do, but this doesn't always make sense. Simple is best.

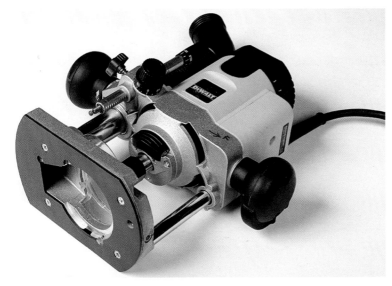

This squared-off base casting is a typical plunge router configuration. Fixed-base castings are round. The polished tubes and plunge bearings in the DeWalt 621 provide the tool with a smooth plunge action.

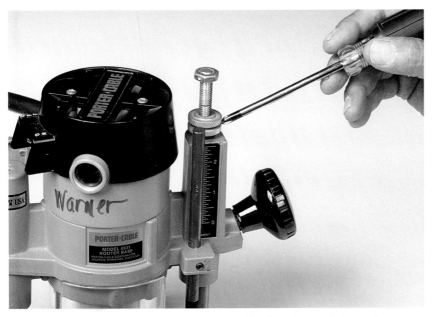

The up-stop on this Porter-Cable 6931 can be used with a fine-adjust knob for continuous adjustment. It also can be set so you know the cutter is clear of the work when the head is up.

The plunge router's essential advantage is its ability to start up with the cutter retracted and stab into the workpiece in a controlled fashion. Thereafter, it can remove the remaining stock in equal passes, changing depth, and cleaning up its mess (in many cases), all while its motor is running. What could be sweeter?

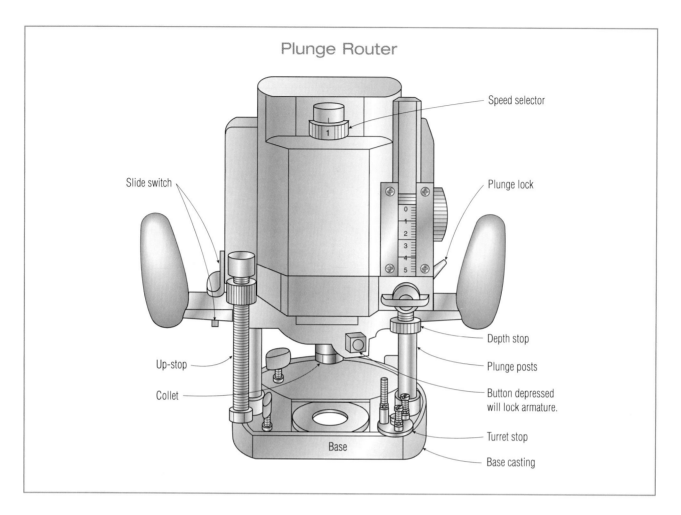

Plunge Router

- Speed selector
- Slide switch
- Plunge lock
- Up-stop
- Collet
- Depth stop
- Plunge posts
- Button depressed will lock armature.
- Turret stop
- Base
- Base casting

Basic Anatomy

Plunge routers lack the designer's touch. The machines are designed for function, not looks. And although they have common features, the manufacturers use a variety of ways to the put the components together.

MOTOR HEAD

The motor head is a combination of aluminum and reinforced engineering plastic. The head is the heaviest component of the router and is the reason for its tipsiness. The handles, switches, depth mechanisms, motor lock, speed controls, and motor are all part of the head assembly. The ergonomics of these features and functions differ somewhat from router to router. What is reasonable and comfortable for one worker will not suit the next guy. All of the motor head functions are safe and work well within practical limits. I would not rule out any one tool on the basis of a quirky switch or the feel of its handles. There will be things both pleasant and uncomfortable to all of us.

The RT-1800 plunge router from Fein is the newest of at least eight 3-hp machines. It has soft start, variable speed and a 3-in. plunge stroke.

The DeWalt 621, right, has its motor lock in the left-hand knob. Spin it to lock or unlock. The Porter-Cable motor lock, left, is "on" in its default position. A twist of the lever unlocks it.

PLUNGE TUBES

All motor heads are fastened to, locked on, and pogo on a pair of plunge tubes. They are hardened, usually polished, and sometimes covered with protective bellows. If a wrench slips off the collet nut, it will ding a tube and spoil the smooth travel of the motor head. (Some machines now use one of the tubes for chip collection when attached to a vacuum.) The idiosyncrasies of the tubes are not reason enough to accept or reject a router, but their interplay with the motor head and column bearings is. You should carefully check for a smooth action when considering a purchase.

The springs that pogo the router on the posts should be such that they pick the motor head up to its stop in a measured and nearly buoyant fashion. An oversprung motor head—that is, one with too much spring—will prevent a smooth plunge action.

BASE CASTINGS

The base castings of plunge routers are all different sizes and shapes. The reason for such diversity is control. The designers of these devices assumed that a straight section on a base casting could be used against a guide for more control and accuracy. In practice, the subbase/casting is the least accurate and most troublesome method of guiding a router. In fact, these truncated castings along with the elevated motor head are the reason plunge routers are so unwieldy. A round base casting is the best compromise. The Porter-Cable 7539 has the biggest; the DeWalt 621 has one of the worst, which I will address later. Larger, clear plastic "stability" subbases are available for some plunge routers.

The castings receive the plunge tubes; provide a means for collar guide, subbase, and edge-guide attachment; and support the turret stop. They are sometimes also used as funnels for the vacuum systems. The vacuum systems do work, but the hose can get in the way. During production, the hose is sometimes supported from above the worker.

Checking for Smooth Action

Some plunge routers will jam if you plunge down on only one handle, which you can live with. But if compression on both handles does not result in a smooth up and down glide of the head to its full extremes, that router should be left aside.

Plunge-base castings are all different, but they share some instability when routing along the edges of the work. The plunge router, at lower left, has been fitted with an aftermarket round subbase for greater stability.

THE DEWALT 621 has long been the router of choice in midweight plunge routers. This 2-hp, variable-speed, soft-start, 9-lb. machine has an ergonomic design and an excellent plunge action. Its plunge stroke, at 2¼ in., is a bit shorter than some routers, but substantial nonetheless.

The DeWalt has a two-stage depth adjuster on a rack-and-pinion gear. The fine adjuster is a screw "pencil" within the coarse adjuster. Adjustments to a few thousandths of an inch are possible. However, a lock to prevent slipping while routing would be an improvement.

Also standard with the 621 is integrated chip-collection capability. The base casting, vacuum funnel, and its exhaust tube (doubling as a plunge tube) were engineered as a package, not an afterthought. The system works very well on inside cuts, the main arena for the plunge router. Hauling a hose as you rout is not great fun, but it's better than getting MDF in your eye.

The 621 has a spindle lock so only one wrench is needed to change bits, but this has its drawbacks. The router must lie on its side for the cutter change; it will not sit upside down. It is easier to accidentally bash one of the plunge posts with a slipped spindle wrench than if you have two wrenches grasped in one hand opposing one another.

The double-insulated router has an 8-ft. wire set that's short for a 6-ft. person. Also, its short subbase axis is in the direction of travel so that the tool can easily tip if the cutter is deeply engaged in the work. An aftermarket large-diameter subbase is available for the 621 that will help keep it flat on the work.

One common feature that's lacking in this plunge router is a stop to limit the upward travel.

DeWalt 621	
Weight	9 lbs.
Speed	Variable, 8,000–24,000 rpm
Amps	10
Soft start	Yes
Horsepower	2.0
Collets	¼ in. & ½ in.
Baseplate diameter	4⁵⁄₁₆-in. x 6¼-in. cutter hole offset
Plunge stroke	2¼ in.

DeWalt 621

Power as an Asset

I think plunge routers do their best work on inside cuts doing multistage work like mortising—jobs they were designed for. A plunge router can approach an inside cut under power, not tip, and waste away stock in stages of an ⅛ in. or so in seconds. Three or four quick passes and you're ½ in. to ¾ in. deep. A cut that deep would break a lot of router bits in a fixed-base tool. A ³⁄₁₆-in.-deep cut with a ½-in.- or ¾-in.-diameter straight bit and a 10-amp tool is a cakewalk with a plunge router. With more power you can do it faster and take deeper cuts but not much more; the cutters can't take it. Consequently, for a lot of plunging, much more than 2 hp is wasted.

Plunge routers range from 1 hp to 3 hp and from 5 lbs. to 17 lbs. The heavier plunge routers are often in the router table, working against gravity, and usually not in the hands of the woodworker for which they were designed. The midweights are the most popular of the plunge routers to be used with jigs, edge guides, and so on, and consequently are the most visible in portable use.

Adding Stability

All routers, whether fixed-base or plunge, are stable when their base castings are surrounded by the work. They will require more skill to handle when less than half the casting is on the work, as is the case with edge cuttings. The plunge router tends to tip more on edges than the fixed-base. As mentioned before, the reasons for that are simple. The motor head rests high on the plunge tubes, the handles are far apart (10 in. to 12 in. or more) and the base castings are light in weight and frequently truncated. Plunging with only half the router on the work is risky.

Wherever the plunge router is stable, whether in fixture or simply on solid ground, it's a safe tool. Releasing the motor lock, plunging, locking, and routing another pass is easy to learn and fun to do. The components to do this vary from tool to tool, and their comfort and efficiency in your hands is a matter of preference. I have tried most plunge routers and can manage them all. For me, the most sensible and comfortable system is embodied in the DeWalt 621. The armored ball knobs each have two functions, which in turn always keep your hands on the knobs. The right hand is for plunge control and switching, and the left is also for plunge control—but a twist of this knob locks the motor head.

Helpful Features

The result of so many different plunge routers is much diversity and novelty. This section discusses the different features and their importance.

ELECTRIC BRAKE

Two plunge routers include an electric brake: the Makita 3612C and Porter-Cable 7529. This is a good option, because accidents do occur on deceleration. I have broken cutters and ruined jigs, fixtures, and the work itself on deceleration. I probably have done more damage with the switch off and the cutter slowing down than most people have done under power. In my view, all routers should have an electric brake.

PROTECTIVE PLUNGE-TUBE BELLOWS

Bellows seem like a good idea; they protect the posts from impact damage and preserve lubricant. The Freud FT2000E and Bosch 1613 use them. Other routers, notably the DeWalt 621 and 625, work endlessly without them.

Increasing Stability

Most plunge routers have relatively small subbases and tend to tip. You can easily increase the stability by making a larger, ¼-in.-thick, round subbase from clear plastic. Transfer the mounting hole locations from the existing subbase to make it any convenient size.

CHIP COLLECTION CAPABILITY

Integrated vacuum collection systems are a good idea. The DeWalt 621 and 625 and the Porter-Cable 7529 (and other Porter-Cable routers) are "vacuum ready." Aftermarket vacuum accessories are becoming common. Chip and dust collection are not only important for our health, but the quality of work can improve, too. A recut chip wears on the cutter and "fouls the footway" in tight quarters, especially with template mortising. Collars and bearings transmit edge and template defects into the work. If a bearing rolls over a chip, it can cause a bump on the work. The vacuum hose is troublesome but better than a chattered profile. Some work, especially with plastics, will require exhaust right at the cutter.

REMOVABLE HANDLES

For hand control, grips are essential. For router table use, they are unnecessary. The DeWalt 625 and Freud FT2000, for example, have removable handles for easier installation. The Hitachi plunge routers all have handles that pivot.

220 VOLTS

The only plunge router with 220 volts is the Bosch 1615 and it is soon to be phased out. The 2-hp Bosch 1617 (fixed-base) has a 220-volt option. Routers with 110 volts are capable of heavy work, but they are not production tools. Sometimes they are used in production work, but the equivalent operation is usually done on the shaper if hours or shifts of the same operation are called for. Short, very heavy-duty cuttings are likely to burn out a standard router; the 220-volt tool will run cooler longer, which is its essential benefit.

Even if shaper power and durability were available in a router, the present-day $\frac{1}{2}$-in. shank tools couldn't stand the stress. The power to take a deeper cut at a higher feed rate is nice, but the limiting factor is the cutters, which are likely to break.

SPINDLE LOCK

Spindle locks are found on most plunge routers. In my view, the two-wrench systems are easier and less likely to cause accidental harm to the router and to the "squeezer." I suspect their presence on plunge routers is more for marketing purposes than practicality. How else can you explain their absence on fixed-base tools?

COLLETS

All routers have collets. A cutter seizing in the collet used to be an ordinary experience. But today essentially all routers use multisplit self-releasing designs. They all let go of their cutters handily on demand and hold the cutter tight. Not much can be said about collets except keep them clean (inside and out) and throw them away every 300 hours to 500 hours or so, or immediately if a cutter slips in one.

Preventing Theft

Some shops use a 220-volt router as a means to prevent theft on the theory that most potential thieves won't have the right electrical outlet to use the tool.

This offset subplate can be used with Porter-Cable collar guides.

These collets are similar. Mark them so you won't accidentally put one in the wrong router. Since the collets are captured on their nut, they pull out of the armature and never stick in the router.

Best Uses for Plunge Routers

Clearly, a plunge router can be used wherever the fixed-base router can, but the fixed-base router poses some risks to the operator in applications where the plunge router does its best work. We have already established that the plunge router is handicapped doing edge work, so what can it do best?

MORTISING

Mortising with a fixed base is rarely practical or safe. A plunge stab with a fixed base and cutter extended may cause the router to self-feed or break the cutter. A plunge router is the best tool for mortises. For speed and accuracy, a jig should be used with an edge guide on both sides of the work and jig (see chapter 9). Mortise depths to about 2½ in. are the practical limits, although given two plunge routers with the same setup, 3 in. or more are possible without having to change any cutters.

CIRCLES AND ELLIPSES

Cutting a circle is generally a multistage task, so a plunge router works well because it can be lowered gradually to cut through the stock. A template is often the first stage of the process and the template then is used on the work with trim cutters. A template can be cut out of an MDF or plywood blank. A disk or oval will break out of the blank on the final pass. It should be screwed down onto another substrate to prevent it from vibrating against the cutter. Fastening a plunge router to a circle or ellipse jig is the most accurate and least costly of methods when making these shapes. A bandsaw can be used more efficiently, but not to the precision or finish quality of a router and straight bit.

HALF LAPS, SLOTS, AND TENONS

Slotting, lapping, and tenoning are user-specific operations. There are no textbook standards for these chores. For me, all three are multistage.

You can rout from both sides of the work when making a disk or hole. Obviously, use the same pivot hole. If you leave a thin membrane, you can just snap it out of the blank.

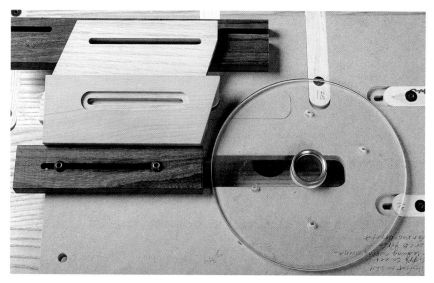

Full-thickness slots are multistage cuts. The work is clamped below the window where the collar guide is sitting. A sample is shown on the jig. There is plenty of platform support for the router.

The tenon-making jig with a window and a broad ski allows you to cut tenons deeper than the ⅝-in. bit. To make a 1½-in. tenon, use the plunge router for progressively deeper cuts. The bearing sets the depth of cut and establishes the shoulder of the tenon.

Cutters are just too short, often too fragile, and the work too demanding or dangerous for a fixed-base tool in one pass. I've made jigs to accommodate and support the plunge router in each case.

CUTTER-BREAKING TROUBLES

The most important time to use a plunge router is when the cut is deep or large enough to risk breaking the cutter. If the depth of cut is such that a single pass of the tool will break the cutter, or burn it out, then a plunge router is called for. Even edge work can fall into this category. Any time the cut will require two passes, it's best to rig the operation to use a plunge router, even if that means building up support on the outboard side of the base to prevent tipping.

Edge work here also refers to the edge of templates (and dovetail jigs are templates). Dovetail bits are single-depth cutters by design; they can't be used at two depths on the same center. The dovetail bit is one of the most fragile and easiest to break. If its pathway is partly cleared by a pre-plow from a straight bit, the dovetail cutter has an easier time and is less likely to chatter. A plunge router can pare away the pathway in two or three steps with a straight bit and do it quickly. I would use the plunge

The use of this ¾-in.-radius roundover bit limits the amount of base casting on the work during startup to less than 40 percent, so I screwed an equal thickness stick to the casting for support.

router in this "utility" function without hesitation, its instability notwithstanding. Moreover, any cutting error from the straight bit will be completely erased by the dovetail bit. For the best dovetail cuttings try to preplow with the next smaller dovetail bit rather than a straight bit.

ROUTER TABLE USE

Plunge routers are probably the most popular choice for router tables, especially for heavy use. This is mainly because there are more choices in the 3-hp range than with fixed-base routers. They're also relatively inexpensive—as 3-hp routers go.

But the choice does present several problems. Since the plunge router motor head is inseparable from the rest of the router, you can't change the bit easily if the tool is bolted right to the tabletop. Consequently, most folks compromise by attaching the plunge router to a big piece of plastic or metal that's inset into the tabletop. The whole assembly is removed for bit changes.

In my view, this compromises the routing process as well as the tabletop integrity and flatness. Inevitably, the top will cup up slightly and so will the plastic insert. Expect interruptions as the work bumps into the transitions where the plastic meets the top. Moreover, expect the plastic to deflect as you press the work down and against the cutter. Close work will be frustrated when a table has the insert construction. It's not so much the plunge router being in the table; it will work, but it is the insert and its installation that are problematic. I prefer a fixed-base router bolted directly to the underside of the router table top.

Porter-Cable 7529	
Weight	11 lbs.
Speed	Variable, 10,000–23,000 rpm
Amps	12
Soft start	Yes
Horsepower	2
Collets	¼ in., ½ in., ⅜ in., & metrics option
Baseplate diameter	6½ in.
Plunge stroke	2½ in.

Porter-Cable 7529

Porter-Cable 7529

The Porter-Cable 7529 plunge router is new in the U.S. market and designed to compete with the best of them.

For openers, the Porter-Cable has a hefty plunge stroke (2%6 in. total) and a large, stable base casting with a round subbase. The Porter-Cable has an up-stop that does double duty as a full range microadjuster in both directions of travel. The 7529 also has a spindle lock, but the company's standard pair of wrenches can also be used.

This double-insulated, 2-hp, variable-speed, soft-start tool also has an electronic brake, an important safety feature. It has a relatively quiet and well-balanced motor, with a 10-ft. power cord.

The armored ergonomic grips are close to the controls. One control, the depth stop, can be adjusted with the left hand while holding the grip— all the while maintaining control of the router, a Porter-Cable exclusive.

The depth stop on the Porter-Cable 7529 can be worked while your left hand is still on the grip, a smart safety move.

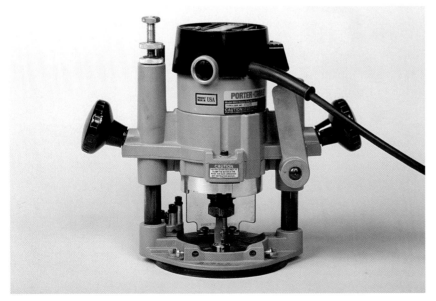

The Porter-Cable 6931 plunge router.

Porter-Cable has also designed the base casting as a vacuum funnel with a connection for a 1-in. vacuum hose. Collectors are also available for edge trimmings, which are harder to pick up.

The variable-speed selector is safely out of the way, but is difficult to rotate. The tool has two switches with thermal overload protection, but I have trouble with the trigger switch coordinating the two steps to lock it on. The plunge glide is acceptable, but the head will jam if downward pressure is only applied to one knob. The tool is heavy at 11 lbs. and much wider than it is thick, making it unstable—but less so than most.

Another plus is that Porter-Cable has designed this tool for router table or hand use with a mechanism that provides for continuous adjustment either upside down or right side up.

Porter-Cable also has two other plunge routers. The 6931 plunge router is essentially the 691 fixed-base router with a plunge base. The 7538 and 7539 are plunge versions of the Speedmatic 3¼-hp fixed-base routers.

DeWalt 625

The industry standard in the heavyweight class is DW-625, formerly the Elu 3338. Like all routers, it is not perfect but deserves its position as the best big plunge router. Its controls are well situated and function smartly. The plunge glide, as on the DW-621, is as good as it gets. The maximum plunge depth is 2⁷⁄₁₆ in. Its features are otherwise unremarkable except for its conspicuous up-stop. It limits the up-travel and functions as the fine adjustment knob.

The 625 is a double-insulated, 3-hp, variable-speed, soft-start, 13.3-lbs. tool. It has a spindle lock for one-wrench cutter changes, a two-stage depth adjuster, and a trigger switch with a lock. It's a good tool.

It suffers from the usual plunge router instability problems because the base is so small, but an offset subbase will keep the tool flat on the work. Also, its base casting is truncated and the cutter opening is so wide that it can snag on the corners of the work. Another minor problem is that the action of the up-stop quick release button is stubborn.

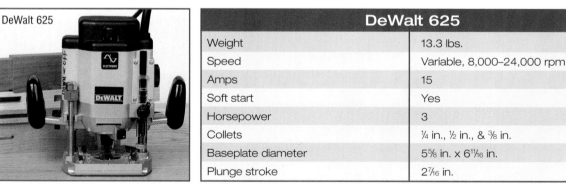

DeWalt 625

DeWalt 625	
Weight	13.3 lbs.
Speed	Variable, 8,000–24,000 rpm
Amps	15
Soft start	Yes
Horsepower	3
Collets	¼ in., ½ in., & ⅜ in.
Baseplate diameter	5⅝ in. x 6¹¹⁄₁₆ in.
Plunge stroke	2⁷⁄₁₆ in.

Laminate Trim Routers

L aminate trim routers are essentially small routers designed for light-duty chores. They have ¼-in. collets, range from ½ hp to 1 hp, and generally weigh 3 lbs. to 4 lbs. They spin fast (25,000 rpm to 30,000 rpm) but use short trim cutters. With a small diameter to match the shank size, these cutters don't generally have balance problems at this high speed.

The field has grown to the point where there are quite a few choices, including Porter-Cable, DeWalt, Bosch, Hitachi, Makita, Ryobi and Freud. Porter-Cable has three different models, so there are at least nine choices. The DeWalt, Bosch and Porter-Cable trimmers can be supplemented with tilting or offset-base castings. These will allow specialty operations such as scribing a countertop to a wall with the counter in place. The Hitachi standard base will tilt 0 to 45 degrees.

Guide Systems

In a way, the variety of laminate cutting systems is a bit surprising. They range from simple ball-bearing guides to aftermarket micrometer-type systems such as the Micro Fence guide with precision micrometer adjustment.

The ball-bearing-guided trim cutter may be the simplest method of trimming laminate flush to its substrate. The standard flush-trim bit has the bearing at the bottom of the cutter, but the top-mounted bearing is

This Bosch Model 1609A offset trim router has the cutter off to one side so it can trim closer to an inside corner and scribe the wall profile onto a countertop or back splash.

The tilting-base Hitachi Model TR6 trim router can be used when the edges of the substrate are at an angle. It can also be used with an edge guide and straight bit to bevel with a straight cutter.

Top-bearing pattern bits used with trim routers are excellent for template routing jobs such as small hinge mortises.

increasingly popular. The Achilles' heel of the ball-bearing trim router is the bearing. Small bearings at high speed just don't last very long. You may get as little as an hour or so of cumulative use before the bearing runs out of lubrication and fails to spin properly.

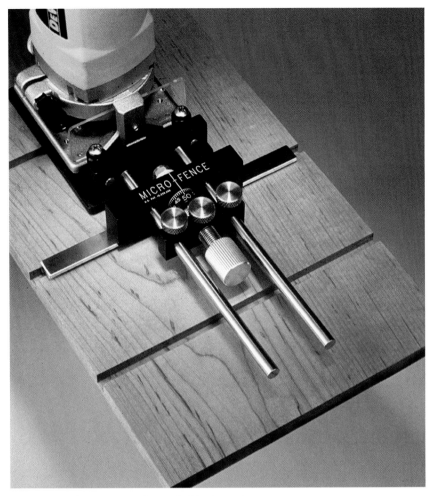

Micro Fence edge guides can be used with trim routers.

THE SUBBASE GUIDE BEARING

Most trimmers have an accessory roller-bearing glide assembly that fastens
to the subbase. Its position, relative to the cutter, can be adjusted somewhat for a measured offset from the cutter. (The cutter's diameter should
reside just inside the diameter of the bearing.) The essential advantage of
this setup is bearing life and cut quality. The bearing rolls at the feed rate
of the router, so it never spins fast enough to burn out.

Another advantage is the bearing's isolation. It's separate from the cutter and armature, so it doesn't vibrate with them. Moreover, any excess
side forces of the tool against the work are transferred to the subbase, not
the armature. These factors result in less chatter, smoother cuts, and longer
motor and bearing life. It all sounds pretty rational, but in reality replacing
$3 bearings on a trim-router cutter once a week of steady use is not all that
terrible of an alternative to the guide bearing described above.

Ball-bearing-guided bits can be expected to trim about 1,200 ft. off countertops at a feed rate of 20 ft. per minute. That's about 120 average-length countertops.

Most trim routers have these accessory roller guides available. Since the bearings don't spin at the rate of the router, they last a long time.

Solid carbide bits can trim and bevel simultaneously, and are surprisingly inexpensive. However, they leave skid marks on the edges of the work.

SOLID TRIM CUTTERS

A third method of trimming laminate is with solid carbide trim cutters and no bearings. These ¼-in. tools are ground to flush and/or bevel cut as shown above. However, the end of the tool skids on the work and may scratch it. For utility surfaces it's an economical choice. I would also use these bits with wood veneer that will be sanded.

EDGE GUIDES

In place of (or in addition to) ball bearings, some manufacturers make simple plastic edge guides that fasten to the subbase. The edge guide has the advantage of continuous adjustability, and the side pressure is transferred to the casting or subbase instead of the cutter or armature. Chips can trap themselves between the edge-guide surface and the work and scratch it. Edge guides can also be made to nest in curved surfaces. With an edge guide you have more cutter choices, but carbide is essential with plastic laminate.

The Industry Standard

THE PORTER-CABLE 310 HAS LONG held its position as the industry standard in trim routers. It has been in production for over 25 years, previously under the Rockwell name. This quiet (27,000 rpm), 4-amp, 3.75-lb., squat router is hand-sized and the least top-heavy of trimmers. With its spiral ground motor lifted by the depth ring, cutter height changes are easy, and travel greater than 1 in. is possible. The round motor-lock knob is not great but acceptable.

Porter-Cable 310

Tilting and offset-base castings are no longer available for the 310. A two-wrench collet lockup (no spindle lock) is rather convenient. I'd recommend a larger, transparent offset or round subbase for this router.

As edge-only tools, all trim routers are unstable, and the 310 is no exception. Its slide switch is exposed and vulnerable to an accidental start. Cutter visibility is from one side only because its motor is centered in its windowed casting and is not cantilevered like the Bosch and others.

Porter-Cable 310	
Weight	3.75 lbs.
Speed	Single speed: 27,500 rpm
Amps	4
Soft start	No
Horsepower	About ⅝
Height adjuster/mechanism	Ring hung, twist ring to 1-in.+ range
Collets	¼ in.
Baseplate diameter	4-in. disk

Other Features and Applications

Trim routers are indeed routers, lest we forget. They accept router bits and guides, spin at about 25,000 rpm to 30,000 rpm, and can rout the same material as big routers. As such, a trim router can be used for general wood and nonferrous metalwork. However, I would never expect industrial-router service from a trim router.

A trim router can be used for hardware mortising. Template cutters like this one have top-mounted bearings to follow the pattern.

The transparent subbase accessory will accept the two-piece Porter-Cable collar guide assembly.

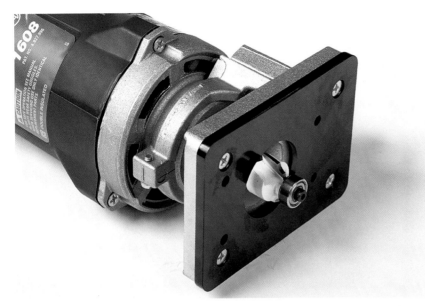

This roundover bit is perfect for knocking off the sharp corners from the planer or jointer.

You can template-rout shallow excavations using top-bearing-guided bits. Also, it's handy that both the Porter-Cable and DeWalt trim routers will accept Porter-Cable collar guides for template work. Small profile cutters are also good for roundovers (up to a radius of ¼ in.), bevels, and V-grooves. But I'd keep the depths of cut very shallow—not more than the equivalent of ³⁄₁₆ in. square.

I know a carver who wastes shallow relief from his blanks before using his chisels. With an edge guide and straight bit you can make wide, shallow, decorative rabbets. There isn't much depth adjustment with trim routers—maybe 1 in. at most. Remember, these tools are designed for trimming, not for timber-frame joinery.

STABILITY AND TRANSPARENCY

You wouldn't think one-handed tools would have stability problems, but they do. The squat designs are more stable, but the tall "Tom Collins" tumbler design is more precarious. A 3-in.- or 4-in.-diameter subbase trim router with a ½-in. cutter has less than 2 sq. in. of contact on the work-piece as it rounds the corner. It will tip. A larger subbase is recommended.

Also, Ryobi and Makita have clear, see-through subbases; all the rest have black bases, and their cutter visibility is poor.

The author's offset subbase provides increased control for edge work, especially around turns and on ends.

Make Life Easier

Use two wrenches to change the bits on trim routers so you don't have to struggle to hold on while trying to turn the wrench.

SPINDLE LOCKS

The spindle lock is sometimes praised as a good feature for router-bit changes. I would rather use two wrenches. A spindle lock on a trim router is unwieldy; the motors are so small that you can't hold them when using a single wrench. However, cutters aren't changed that often in the trim router.

DEPTH OF CUT CHANGES

The cutter depth when trimming plastic laminate is not critical. Plus or minus $\frac{1}{8}$ in. is easily tolerable and required to distribute the wear over the length of the flute. Since there isn't much demand for a precise depth of cut, fancy depth changers are not found on most trim routers. The one exception is the Porter-Cable 310, which you can adjust very accurately. The motor is hung on a depth ring that evenly supports it. A turn of the calibrated ring raises or lowers the bit in a precise and measured way. Cantilevered motor/casting designs with screw lifts tend to jam unless you support the motor with your free hand as you change depth settings.

Bosch 1608	
Weight	3.5 lbs.
Speed	30,000 rpm
Amps	5.6
Soft start	No
Horsepower	About $\frac{7}{8}$
Height adjuster/mechanism	Screw-in vise slide, $\frac{1}{2}$-in. range
Collets	$\frac{1}{4}$ in.
Baseplate diameter	$2\frac{3}{4}$-in. x $2\frac{3}{8}$-in. rectangle

BOSCH 1608

Bosch 1608

The Bosch 1608 trim router, at 5.6 amps and 3.5 lbs., is light and powerful—and with its shielded switch you can't accidentally fire it. Its up-and-down mechanism is better than most with $\frac{1}{2}$ in. of screw-driven depth adjustment. The collet is split three ways and holds its cutters well. It is tightened with one wrench, while the armature is held with another wrench near the top of the tool. Its rectangular subbase casting is stable, but no more so than a round one. The tool could benefit from a larger or offset subbase. The motor is interchangeable with offset, tilting, and under-scribe bases.

Router Tables

A router table can handle most routing procedures, but not all of them safely and efficiently. The router table has a big advantage whenever its broad control surfaces (fence and top) are required. The table's most efficient use employs the wide surfaces to support the workpiece for edge routing. The most difficult operation on a table is routing on the ends of long, narrow sticks like stiles and rails. But even difficult jobs can often be safely accomplished by using jigs and fixtures designed to securely hold the workpiece and keep your hands safely away from the cutter. But it's also important to remember that a hand-held router can be the best solution, especially for large or awkward workpieces.

And, as with all router operations, never forget that the spinning cutter is unforgiving and provides no second chances.

A router table can range from the simple to the ridiculously complex; most are over-engineered. For some people, a production-made plastic-laminate table will do. For others, a handmade, job-specific contraption is better. To be sure, a good table with basic features does take time to make well if you build your own.

Router Table Basics

The router table has lots of applications, but it does have its limitations. You can rout short or odd shapes otherwise unsafe to rout with the hand router, but you can't rout big, wide, long sticks or anything so big it might tip the table over. Edges and faces of narrow workpieces are easily routed,

The author's router table has an MDF top that's supported by a series of ribs underneath. He uses a fixed-base router so he can permanently attach the casting and remove the router motor for bit changes.

but a table isn't appropriate for working on the ends. Fortunately, in those cases where the router table is not suitable, a hand-held router will do the job. Nevertheless, 70 percent to 80 percent of all jobs can be safely and accurately routed on the table.

Table routing is often more efficient than hand routing. Most of the work needn't be clamped or worked with a fixture; a fence with a vacuum system will keep the table clean. Adjustments are easy and setup is quick. The same stick or panel can often be routed on its edges, faces, or ends with no changes in setup. An enclosed router table is also relatively quiet.

Since the work can be fed just as easily on its edge or face, a cutter may have more application on the router table than in the hand router.

I made this fence for chamfering the edges of round subbases. The work rolls on two ½-in. bearings and the depth of cut is determined by raising or lowering the cutter.

Using a fence with a cutter allows you to use more of the cutting surface. The ball-bearing design restricts cutting to a small portion of the edge. By raising this cutter and positioning the fence I can use a section of the cutter that has not yet seen any wood.

A 30-degree bevel cutter, for example, can produce a 60-degree bevel if the work is fed on edge. The fence and cutter height can also be adjusted so any part of the flute can be used to better distribute the wear. The same piloted cutter in the hand router will wear out its flutes near the bearing, leaving sharp carbide near the shank.

A router table can be a platform for routing with piloted bits and collars, or you can use the fence. Most cuttings on the table use the fence, and as such no ball bearings are needed on the cutters. The same cutter without a bearing is often smaller and safer, but not necessarily cheaper. When cutter bearings are absent and the fence receives all of the horizontal force from the work, the router and bit are under less stress and last longer. Moreover, when bearings are not used, edge defects are not telegraphed back into the profile, and in general router fence cuttings are crisper, with less chatter.

THE STAND

A typical router table has a stand, top, and fence. The stand's essential function is to bring the height of the work up to a comfortable level. It should also provide a means for supporting, flattening and attaching the top. Material (usually MDF) and rigidity will inhibit vibration and contain noise. A stand made from ¼-in. plywood and 1-in. by 1-in. legs will support a router. But a stand with 2-in. by 2-in. legs, 1½-in. by 2½-in. rails, and ⅝-in.-thick MDF will be stronger and support the components in the subassemblies.

A router stand should be like the stands for jointers, planers and bandsaws: no drawers or storage, maybe an access door, and a place for electrical equipment. It should be strong enough to be pulled around without coming apart. I am not opposed to casters, either permanent or detachable. I have a wire winder in mine, as well as an 18-in. straightedge and a ⅜-in. shoulder bolt to lock a set of spacers on the top to lift the work to various heights in relation to the bit.

A 15-amp rocker switch buried in a mortise prevents accidental startups, but is easy to shut off.

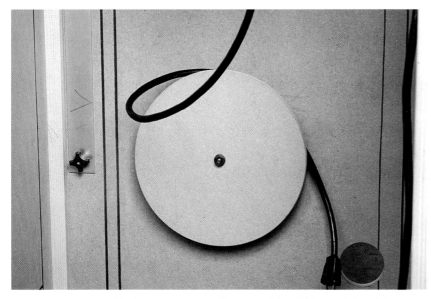

The wire winder can hold about 18 ft. of wire. There is a 6-in. disk beneath the 10-in. one you see. The straightedge at left comes in handy for setups.

The router table box rests on four 1-in. ball casters that are screwed into threaded brass inserts. Two Lexan brakes keep the 80-lb. box from rolling away.

I use a 2-ft.-wide by 2-ft.-deep by 39-in.-high stand. It can just manage a hefty 6-ft. board, which is also my physical limit, so I wouldn't need a bigger stand. The bigger these things get, the heavier they get—and the more likely they are to warp.

Router work is not like chiseling or other common woodworking activity. You should not expect most shop furniture to be at the optimum height for routing. I'm 6 ft. tall and all my routing surfaces are high—about 38 in. to 44 in.

Obviously, the stand is used as the support for the top. As such, you should put some framing into the upper rails to support and connect it. My table has six upper rails that I struggled to get into the same plane. They provide the means to keep the top flat so the top itself can be as thin as is practical.

The material, design and thickness of the top depend somewhat on the router table design and whether a fixed-base or plunge router is used. But before I address that, I would like to present my case for a fixed-base router in the table. Using a fixed base simplifies the top and improves routing accuracy.

FIXED-BASE OR PLUNGE

Although both types of tools are used in router tables, I prefer to use a fixed-based rather than a plunge router. One reason for that is that it's not practical to bolt a plunge router to the underside of the table. Its motor is permanently fastened to the casting, so cutter changes upside down are complicated. Most people screw the plunge router to large metal or plastic subbases, which in turn are nested into rabbeted windows within the top.

Router Table Height

You can use the adjustable table of a drill press to determine the most comfortable router table height. Try clamping a straightedge (to simulate a router table fence) on the drill press table and run pieces of various sizes over the setup. Try the procedures at heights from 36 in. to 42 in. and build to the height that works best. Safety note: Do not rout on the drill press, just go through the motions.

With this arrangement, cutter and depth changes can be made, since the router can now be easily extracted. Nevertheless, that one maneuver brings about one compromise after another. For example, the tops themselves get overly complicated with tee-moldings or laminations of fiberboard, plywood, or particleboard. The window has to be a precise match for the large subbase, and the absence of a third of the top (for the window) will spoil its integrity and promote cupping and twisting in what is left.

Moreover, the edges where the insert plate and tabletop meet become dust collectors and need constant cleaning to prevent the work from hanging up. Precision work will be more difficult because the plastic insert can bend with downward pressure, causing small changes in depth of cut. Every time you pull the router and insert out of the table, you need to level and inspect the rabbet seat and insert for a good fit. A fixed-base casting bolted directly onto an MDF top has none of these problems. You simply remove the router motor from the casting to change the bit.

Simplicity, again, is always the best option. This does limit your router choices, however. For serious router table work such as raising panels, you may need a 3-hp machine—and there are many more available as plunge routers than as fixed-base routers. However, the Porter-Cable model 7518 does fill that bill. For lighter-duty router tables, there are a host of machines in the various power categories.

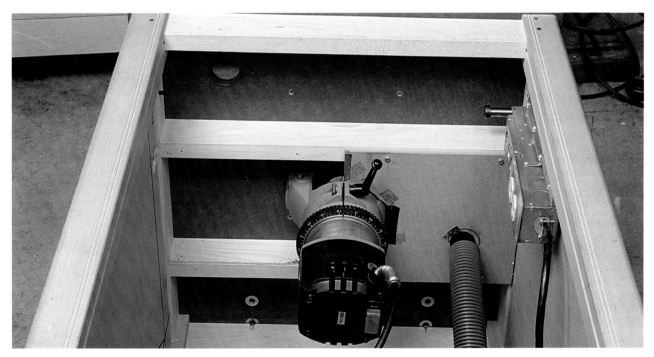

The hefty supports underneath the top ensure that the MDF panel stays flat—a key consideration for router table design.

TABLETOP MATERIAL

Given the fixed-base option, then, the material of choice is MDF—thin (⅝ in.) MDF if your table is stressed with reinforcing rails. Cabinet-grade MDF (such as Medite brand) is finish-sanded to a uniform thickness. This untreated surface will wear and scratch easily. However, two or three coats of Watco will impart a Masonite-like toughness to it and do no harm. It will not be as tough as plastic laminate, but it will resist wear and last a long time. What could be easier?

I would not expect to use cutter-hole inserts for the same reasons I wouldn't use a baseplate insert. A 2-ft. by 2-ft. by ⅝-in. MDF slab is about $2, so it's better to make a spare than degrade either one with an insert. Make one with a hole for your biggest cutter and one with a cutter hole for general use, exchanging them as necessary.

MDF can be bolted down on a table frame without dimensional consequence; no allowance is necessary for changes in humidity or temperature. I would minimize overhang, though, as unsupported surface can cup.

This top has seen hundreds of hours of routing with little wear. Flatness along the cutter path remains within 0.002 in.

A dial indicator on a router table fence may be overkill, but for precise joinery it can save precious time.

The Fence

The fence is the most critical element of a router table. Ideally, it should be straight and square to the tabletop. A stick on a pivot will do, but for speedier adjustments, a split fence with a screw-driven adjustment is better. Also note that making a precise router fence is much easier if you already have a fence. So you may want to find a good straight board to use for a starter fence. Moreover, even the most comprehensive and sophisticated of fences may not be compatible with all cutters. For example, it may not make sense to over-complicate the design of your fence for the occasional use of a 3½-in.-diameter panel bit. Instead, you can make a second, much simpler, fence with a 3½-in. cutout for that operation.

The router fence has two essential functions: One is to guide your stick by the cutter and the other is to regulate the horizontal depth of cut. The guidance function, as implied, is not that difficult to design into the

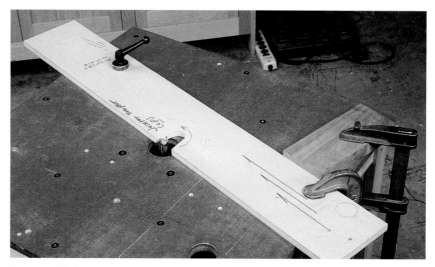

A router table fence can be as simple as a pivot stick and a couple of clamps.

The author's router table fence is driven with a machine screw. The 1-in. aluminum bars fit into ways cut into the bottom of the fence so that it tracks straight and doesn't twist.

fence; a well-jointed stick will do that. The depth-of-cut function is also easy to manage, but it is more of a challenge and is often overlooked.

Router bits, horsepower and the nature of wood are usually in such conflict that the desired full depth of cut is not possible in a single pass (the easiest way to manage this problem is with an adjustable fence). I know of three methods of moving a fence: the tap and clamp, the pivot, and the screw drive. The first and simplest fence is clamped to the table and tapped with a hammer for adjustment. It's unsophisticated, unrepeat-able, and frustrating—but it's the most common method. The second system uses a stick with a pivot so only one clamp is needed. (Stops and screws can be used to advantage here.) The third method and the least common incorporates a lead-screw to drive the fence. My own is assembled on a carrier through which a couple of clamp levers secure the whole thing. The levers are coupled to tee-nuts beneath the top.

Protection from the Cutter

A router bit is an unforgiving cutting tool. One of the safety features of a router table is that most of the time the cutter is buried in the stock or behind the fence, so you are protected from it. If your fence is split, it's good practice to minimize the cutter opening to reduce the cutter exposure. When routing full thickness, allow only $\frac{1}{16}$ in. or so of cutter above the stock, again to hide as much tool as possible. Plastic cutter guards are valuable in some circumstances, and you should use one if you need more protection. For me, if I think a plastic cutter guard is necessary, then I know I'm at risk, and I work out an alternate routing strategy to minimize it. If the work is too narrow, short, or peculiar, or puts my hands too close to the bit, I'll build a holder or a special utility fence.

A router fence has a number of uses besides the usual functions, such as guiding the stock, hiding the cutter and controlling the in-and-out depth of cut. It's also handy for placing a variety of stops and offers a platform for dust-collection equipment. My fence has a vacuum port right behind the cutter, and does an excellent job of picking up the chips. Plastic vacuum accessories for router fences are common (see Resources on p. 180).

Using a straightedge and shims, the author adjusts the outfeed half of the fence for a 0.020-in.-deep cut. The cutter lines up with the outfeed fence to make a full thickness pass for a jointed edge.

Whether your fence is split or not, you can use it for jointing operations and making other full-thickness cuts. With a carbide straight bit you can joint plastic, wood, MDF, plywood, and some nonferrous metals. However, MDF and plastic will ruin HSS jointer knives. The outfeed fence should move in and out about 3/64 in., and if you adjust it parallel to the infeed fence and in line with the highest point of the cutter, it will function like a jointer. It will take a thin slice from the full thickness of the workpiece. You can do the same thing with a one-piece fence by attaching some thin (0.010-in. to 0.0025-in.) metal shims on the fence beyond the cutter. A straightedge placed on the outfeed side should just touch the high point on the cutter.

Open mortises and other "stopped" cuts are easy to do on the router table. Often these cuts are only 2 in. or 3 in. in length, so the outfeed fence can be positioned slightly rearward and out of the way. I made a stop with a slot to slide and lock on the outfeed fence—a nice convenience. It's designed to stay above the table so it won't accumulate a pile of chips.

There are more things you can add to a fence. Several small companies are even making a business out of it. Join-Tech, Wood Haven, and Incra, for example, make fences and accessories for dovetails and box joints. Nonetheless, your fence must always be straight and square to the table to be accurate. My fence faces are unfinished, so I can sand, scrape and true them up. I keep them flat to plus or minus 0.001 in.

The 1½-in. plastic tube is a DeWalt 621 router accessory (328592-00) that comes in handy for chip collection on a router table. A brass (chrome-plated) 1½-in. drain tube is also a good choice.

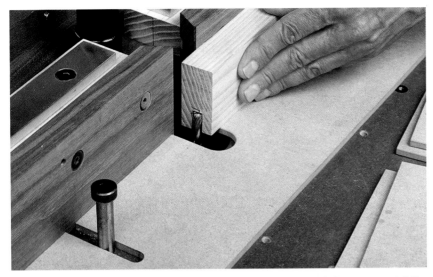

A deep, open mortise like this one, if attempted in one pass, will break the cutter or stall the motor. Routing on ¼-in. lifts solves the problem; remove one for each depth change. The shoulder bolt keeps the lifts from sliding.

I use an 18-in. Starrett ground straightedge to verify the straightness of the fence halves. A 0.0015-in. feeler gauge cannot get under the straightedge.

Depth of Cut Strategies

Material to be cut on the router table must be flat, uniform in thickness, straight and square. That is not a peculiarity; all woodworking machines require it. If your work is cupped, bowed, or otherwise distorted, your cutting results will vary. Given suitable material, a good router table will cut to plus or minus 0.002 in. To cut this close, you need a good fence and a flat tabletop. If any of the three (stock, top, or fence) legs of this triad is less than acceptable, your results will vary.

Router Table or Shaper

THE ROUTER TABLE IS CLEARLY borrowed technology from the shaper. As such, it's a powerful and adaptable tool, but don't expect shaper performance from one.

Both tools are stationary and the operator moves the work, not the tool. Both use fences, collars, or bearings to control the path of the work. But shapers are essentially for edge or end cuttings. They are cabinet-shop and millwork tools and as such are heavy-handed, heavy-duty, and heavyweight. The biggest tool bit in a common router has a ½-in. shank. The smallest spindle on a shaper is ½ in. Moreover, shaper spindles are sophisticated precision-ground components in vibration-dampened, isolated assemblies, separate from their drive motors. In a router the spindle is one and the same with the armature and performs double duty, so its bearings are the first things to wear out.

Shapers are designed for all-day door, drawer, or molding operations. Duty cycles are measured in "shifts," not minutes. They are production animals. Their cutters are big (way over 2 in.) and expensive. Shapers spin slower than routers, usually in the 7,000 rpm to 14,000 rpm range, and their power output starts where routers leave off (around 3 hp).

Router tables sacrifice production for versatility. The router table, unlike the shaper, can do inside work as well as edge, face and end cuttings. Dadoes, mortises and other blind inside excavations are not possible with shapers, nor are dovetails—a distinct argument for the router table.

Router bits for all sorts of woodworking are common, and there are probably more router bits than shaper cutters except for door, drawer, handrail, and window applications. The router is an offshoot of the shaper, not a substitute for one. Its price range is well within the reach of most woodworkers; shapers of any quality start at $1,500.

Router tables are easy to set up, and fill an important need for a wide range of cabinet and furniture applications. They are great for short-run solutions, but as mentioned before, don't expect shaper performance from one.

Controlling a Deep Cut

For a cut that is deep and inside (such as open mortises, dadoes, and grooves) the cutter should be placed at the maximum height. The work should then be routed on a stack of spacers, shown on p. 95, removing one for each depth of cut. Cuttings done this way are safe and precise.

Simplification is another important factor in quality woodworking. The more operations and machine changes, the more chance for error. Obviously, we strive for excellence; good fixtures, good wood, experience and simplification will take us there. To simplify and increase quality control on the router table, any changes in depth of cut have to be well-managed.

VERTICAL DEPTH OF CUT

Often cutters require multiple passes to achieve the desired profile. Sometimes there isn't enough power to get there in one pass; sometimes the cutter can break in a single pass; and sometimes the stock will burn, split, or tear with a heavy cut. If you expect such difficulty, then stage (multiple pass) work is essential. The depth of cut in the router table can be adjusted by the router or the fence. It should be adjusted by one or the other (not both) for a given cutter. Changing both will easily double your chances for a screw-up. Fortunately, the choice of which to manage for a given cutter is easy to make.

HORIZONTAL DEPTH OF CUT

Large-diameter bits are usually short, often intolerant of vertical depth changes, and are used on the edge of stock; to stage-cut with them you move the fence. To do this, set the vertical "depth" to its final position initially and move the fence in equal increments. The diameter of the largest available router bit is around $3\frac{1}{2}$ in.—and $\frac{1}{2}$ in. of that is usually for a bearing. That leaves $1\frac{1}{2}$ in. for the profile, so three or four $\frac{3}{8}$-in. fence changes will complete the cut. Using spacer lifts and fence changes at the same time should be avoided. If you find yourself doing both, you should consider moving up to a shaper.

The sample on the left has a pretty good side wall, but the outside edge of the corner is torn. The sample on the right has been climb cut (fed left to right) but only about $\frac{1}{32}$ in.

I use this sled holder if the work is too narrow or too deep to work safely. I hold the sled by the toggles.

Climb Cutting

The conventional and safe work-feed direction on the router table is from right to left as you face the cutter. In this way, the feed is against the cutter rotation, and as such the work is safely pulled into the fence, covering up the bit. Like planing against the grain, the router bit can cause tearout if the work is fed against the cutter rotation. Sharp cutters and spiral flute design can make this less of a problem, but expect some tearout, especially on difficult woods. Feeding the work from left to right, the climb cut will markedly reduce tearout, but at substantial risk. The climb cut is so named because of the tendency for the router or work to pull (or climb) as you try to feed evenly. The work is constantly being pulled from the hands and away from the fence. This cut is chiefly used for difficult woods in which the grain changes direction. It is less efficient than other cuts, and as such more force is required to control the work. This is risky business. Fortunately, there are counter-measures.

The main use for the climb cut is as a very light "score" made as an initial pass. The light $\frac{1}{32}$-in. depth of cut helps prevent the severe climbing action. Note that you should make a habit of placing the work in a holder that keeps your hands well away from the cutter for climb cuts. Using this technique without such common-sense protection is extremely dangerous. The only time to use a climb cut without a holder is with workpieces that are so large that your hands remain well away from the cutter. In any case, don't take off more than a $\frac{1}{32}$ in. for a single pass.

An MDF work holder is pretty heavy and resistant to power transfers from the cutter in a climb cut. Even if an accident should occur, your hands are on the jig and cannot be pulled into the router bit.

Finally, safe climb cutting can always be done with a power feeder. But you should note that a router table should not be considered a production tool—the very reason for a power feeder. The setup is also technique-sensitive, and your router table has to be a quality one. The feeder will press down hard on the top and against the fence. If either should deflect, your cuttings will vary.

The Miter Gauge

The miter gauge can be useful on the router table, but it's not my favorite choice. I just can't hold the work on one and keep it from slipping. Moreover, most miter-gauge cuts are across the grain and subject to tearout as the cutter exits the work. A back-up waste piece is almost always required—confounding handling even more. A miter slot in the face of the table can weaken it or cause other minor problems. If a miter gauge is needed, a better solution is to use two temporary pieces of $\frac{3}{8}$-in. MDF to trap the blade of the gauge rather than cutting into the top. With this strategy, the fence can remain in play for added work support. A better solution yet is to build a sled fixture with stops and toggle clamps to hold the work (see the photo on p. 100). Well-designed fixtures are imperative for good work, reducing accidents and injuries.

Two pieces of $\frac{3}{8}$-in. MDF clamped to the table provide a temporary pathway for the miter-gauge blade. This method doesn't compromise the router table by cutting into it for a groove.

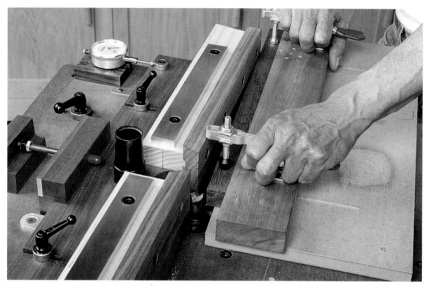

It takes a major calamity to kick this jig out of my hands. Work held in a fixture always machines well.

Router Table Safety

It is clear that high-speed spinning cutters have two possible results: one is to cut the stock; the other is to cut you. There are other threats on the router table, but none as formidable. Safety is an attitude that when followed will improve your efficiency and cutting results. Once in a while, there are genuine surprises but most emergency room visits are due to carelessness. A shoddy setup, difficult wood, inferior machinery, and a fighter-pilot mentality are some of the factors. This book can help you with the unexpected, but not your disposition. And frankly, if you are clumsy, accident prone, and impatient, you should not be a woodworker. The automobile industry has done a yeoman's job of protecting you from yourself and others: air bags, seat restraints, safety glass, and so on. However, the woodworking industry is a work-safety disgrace. Start to believe that, and you will be a conscientious woodworker.

CUTTER SAFETY

Edge routing is the most common table routing practice. You can rout the whole edge or part of it. Either way, there isn't much cutter exposure except at the end of the cut. Routing narrow sticks (2½ in. or less) can be scary because your hands are placed near the cutter for best results. Whenever possible, press down and against the fence beyond the cutter. Should you have a slip, your hands will dash away from the cutter. While paying attention to that maneuver, prepare for the cutter's sudden appearance at the end of the work.

When edge-routing the full thickness—jointing for instance—project only $\frac{1}{16}$ in. of cutter beyond the work. Any more is unnecessary and risky. For best results, match the flute length to the thickness of the work.

Push sticks are always acceptable, but hold-ins, hold-downs, and featherboards can present their own dangers. In my view, they get in the way, upset the uniform travel of the work, and present some risk themselves. To me, they signal that trouble is near; the work is too narrow, too short, too long, or too awkward.

I'm the first to act when it comes to safety. If you see the need for a hold-down or featherboard, then start looking for a jig, fixture, holder, or an alternative method. It could easily be that what you're trying to do is not a table-router operation at all. Some dangerous router table cuts are uncomplicated when done with a fixture and a hand router. And just because you've seen an operation in a book or a magazine, don't assume it's safe. If your results are inconsistent, you don't like doing it, or you are otherwise uncomfortable, you are probably at risk and should consider another method.

Always push down and against the fence *beyond the cutter* when operating a router table.

TRAPPING THE CUTTER AND THE WORK

Because routers generate so much torque, it's crucial to keep the cutters from getting trapped. The work can be trapped between the cutter and the fence or under the cutter. The bit can also be trapped in the work or stuck in the side of the stock. Three of the four situations should be avoided altogether. The fourth is essential to routing and quite common, but done at a risk you should know about.

Trapping the work between the fence and the cutter is about as bad as driving on the wrong side of the road. The question isn't whether an accident will occur, but when. Never set the fence so that the workpiece is sandwiched between it and the cutter. Any slight deviation in stock thickness will jam the workpiece and (very likely) pull your fingers into the bit.

You can also trap the work under the cutter. This is far less common, but the hazards are nearly the same. There is less risk of the work self-feeding, but it will likely ruin the cutter and the work. Be aware: if this happens, it is the result of unsafe practice.

An inside cut like a slot or dado again traps the work between the cutter and the fence. A bad feed or an ill-prepared (poorly jointed edge) workpiece will ruin the cut, may break the cutter, or kick back the work. This is common practice on table-saw dovetail and box-joint jigs and the reason for caution when using a fixture for such a cut. The cutter simply has no place to go in the event of an accident except into an area of the work you didn't want to rout.

The same size dovetail is possible on different thicknesses of stock if both cuts are referenced from the same side of the work. But this strategy should be avoided; it is very risky.

A tongue produced this way—both cuts referenced from the same face of the stock—is high-risk woodworking. If your thickness planer is well-tuned, there is never a need for this.

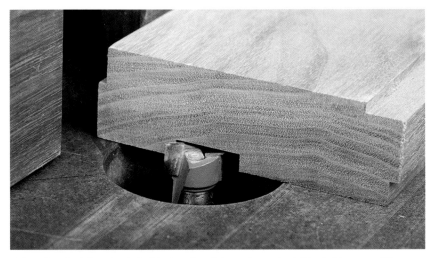

If there is a "safe" method of widening slots it is on the router table. But beware of the surprise climb cut. With the work trapped between the fence and the cutter a bad feed may break the cutter and jettison the work. The safe feed direction to widen the slot is always against the cutter rotation (left to right in this case).

An accidental climb cut can also occur while widening the pathway on inside cuts if you ignore the cutter rotation. Widening the slot as shown in the photo above with a right to left hand feed is a climb cut and will, in all likelihood, rip the work out of your hands. A feed from left to right is not a climb cut but any deviation in workpiece travel can spoil the cut nevertheless.

This door cutter is stuck in the work. If the work is lifted, the cut will be spoiled; if it is bowed or twisted, the panel and rail fit will be compromised and the stick may kick back.

A blind through slot (like on this sample) is a risky act on the router table. The slot was cut with the jig, a collar and a plunge router. The work is clamped under the window.

Some cutters—such as those for slotting and forming glue joints—are buried in the work for normal operation. That is to say, if you lift the work while routing it, you will spoil the cut. Again, you can break a cutter this way and the work can kick back. You need to make sure you never lift the work while using these cutters. Moreover, if the work is bowed, twisted or cupped, its trip down the router table will be tippy and it could jam and fly back at you. Intermittently pressing and relaxing the force down on a bowed workpiece will increase its chances for a kickback. A hold-down may unexpectedly tip the ends up on small work. The best defense against such a calamity is good stock preparation with flat surfaces and square edges.

BLIND-END TABLE CUTS

As mentioned, there are plenty of unsafe but relatively common woodworking practices. The router has its share—maybe more so than the jointer and table saw. Blind-ended cuts are those cuts that begin and end inside the stock and do not exit or enter through the edge. It is possible to do this on the router table, but clearly the cutter is trapped in the work. The heroics go like this: the daredevil first clamps stops down on the router table top, turns on the router, butts the work against the stop, tilts it up, and drops it down on the turning cutter. Next, the operator slides the work to the other stop and lifts it off the table. If successful, said craftsman keeps his afternoon bungee jump appointment.

The above procedure will burn the wood at both ends of the pathway and the slightest waver will ruin the cut on both sides. But the proper alternative is obvious. It is the express purpose of a plunge router to facilitate blind-end cuts. They should be done with the work in a jig or fixture and routed with the portable plunger and edge guide, never on the router table.

Router Bits

It is interesting to note that the purchase of 10 to 15 router bits can easily exceed the dollar value of the most expensive router. These highly engineered carbide router bits can stand four to six regrinds, even though most hobbyist woodworkers rarely sharpen them.

But despite this durable material, a new cutter can and will tear out, break out, or chip out a perfectly good straight-grained piece of wood. The cutter sharpness or geometry doesn't matter nearly as much as a solid understanding of which bit to use—and how to use the bit once you're there.

A few premium cutters can often exceed the price of the router they're used in. These retail for about $227—enough to purchase nearly any 2-hp router.

The cutter is a critical factor. The setup and the type of router are the other two parts of the big picture. All three factors play together in the cutting process. The wrong router, an ill-conceived setup, or a poorly chosen router bit can ruin the work. Working with these variables does take experience, but a closer look at cutters can certainly help the operator make some informed choices.

Evaluating Performance

Manufacturers have a lot to say about router bits. Some of the more common buzzwords are super micro-grain, fatigue-proof steel, spun balanced, anti-kickback, precision ground, optimum hook angles, and Teflon coated. But the bottom line is performance, which can't be predicted from simple inspection or even knowledge of routing. A single manufacturer's cutters can vary in quality, and distributors don't always carry a manufacturer's entire inventory, so selection can be perplexing.

As in other products, a manufacturer's reputation and longevity in the business are reasonable considerations. Very cheap bits should be suspect, since you will "get what you pay for." A good rule of thumb is to select one or two cutters and evaluate their performance. The following will show you how.

FINISH

The finish that a new cutter leaves on wood should be nearly flawless. Rough grinding will telegraph itself onto the work. When used properly you should expect little or no tearout, no burning, and an otherwise smooth and glassy finish. Use the router table to evaluate this; it is the least sensitive to technique.

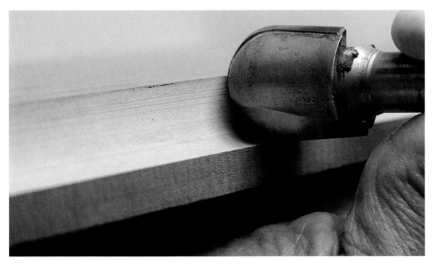

Any grinding defect on a carbide bit will show up plainly on the work.

To check for vibration in a large bit, start it at the slowest of speeds and increase the speed a notch at a time. This PRC trimmer is the longest of all commonly available router bits.

VIBRATION

Vibration is your worst enemy. Clamps loosen, screws unwind, fences squiggle, cutters slide up the collet, and the work can resonate against the cutter. In the worst case, the cutter breaks or comes out of the collet.

Minor vibration of the router bit, once uncommon, seems more and more frequent. But any vibration, in my view, is unacceptable. To test for cutter vibration, use a variable-speed router and start the tool at its slowest speed. Hold the router in the air and advance the speed selector a step at a time. If you feel vibration, stop the router before going to the next speed. (With a hard-start tool you don't have this luxury.)

Cutters whose diameters and flute lengths are less than $1\frac{5}{8}$ in. should spin to 25,000 rpm without vibration. Bigger cutters are far more likely to vibrate even though they are supposed to be in balance beyond 30,000 rpm. Be suspicious of all new big cutters and all newly reground cutters. A bad collet will make most medium-sized cutters vibrate, balanced or not. Bearings, good or bad, may make a bit vibrate, too, so to rule out the cutter as the sole vibrator remove all bearings and screws from the bit.

ACCURACY OF GRIND

Just how close does the manufacturer grind to the stated specification such as radius and diameter? Most makers hold the shank diameter to an extreme tolerance of plus or minus 0.00025 in., but the rest of the tool may vary. For decorative bits, ovolos, beads, and roundovers, for example, it doesn't matter much if a radius is off by a few degrees, but joinery cutters should be more precise. The fit from tongue-and-groove tools, glue-joint cutters, cope-and-stick bits, and dovetails is very sensitive to grinding errors.

Cutter Risk

THE RISKS INVOLVED WITH CUTTERS are very real, but manageable. Although cutters can break, it doesn't often happen when they are used within normal limits. Cutters can also come out of the collet, but not if proper care is taken when inserting and tightening the bit (⅝ in. minimum for ¼-in. bits, ¾ in. minimum for ½-in. bits). Cutters do, of course, present a risk by virtue of their

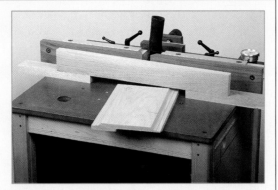

Large bits, such as raised-panel cutters, require extra attention to safety. My "letter slot" fence prevents me from getting my hands close to the cutter no matter what happens.

very sharpness, but careful handling will go a long way toward preventing a cut. And certainly a cut from handling a cutter that's not spinning won't likely send you to the emergency room.

It is true that broken cutters can turn into projectiles, but they rarely do so. They typically break against the stock, so most of their kinetic energy is spent on impact with the work. On occasion, a carbide weld will fail, but that is rare. Safety goggles are a reasonable line of defense. Many dovetail and narrow straight bits often break in a tunnel cut and can't get out, so with these there is little risk. The router sub-base also acts as a shield to cover up the missile.

Adjustment for Bit Wobble

Make some trial cuts in the intended material and adjust your jig to account for the cutter's actual profile. If your spacing between dovetails actually measures, say, 0.76 in. because of cutter deflection—and you want exactly ¾ in.—adjust the spacing on the template to reflect the practical error (in effect, 0.01 in. closer).

The shank of a router bit is held to a very tight tolerance. Rarely is this ever a problem, because the shank has to be the exact diameter to be secured for its own production.

The overall measurements of the router bit are somewhat difficult to establish precisely without elaborate equipment. Top dead center can be difficult to find; the cutter needs to be placed in a special holder or jig, and special measuring gauges are required. A more practical strategy is to measure the work cut by the tool. If your setup is good and your milling is precise, it will be easy to measure your cutting results. For example, a dial

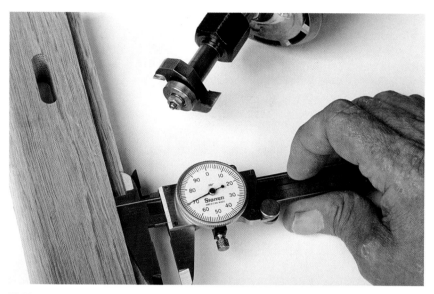

Making a test cut and measuring the results with a set of calipers is a sure-fire way to check the accuracy of a router bit.

Straight cutters come in three primary styles: spiral bits, first and second from left; on shear; and standard straight cutter. The spiral and on-shear bits cut more cleanly than the straight bit.

caliper can measure the depth of a rabbet more easily than it can measure the major and minor diameters of the cutter that made it.

EFFICIENCY

The design and sharpness of the cutting flutes essentially determine the power demand for a bit. Router bits come in a variety of cutting configurations. These include spiral ground, with an up or down pattern to the spiral, and on-shear, where the cutting edge hits the work at a slightly skewed angle. Bits are generally available with two, three, or four flutes. You can assume spiral-ground and on-shear tooling is more efficient. The importance of efficiency is in control. Whether the work is hand fed on the router table or worked with the hand-held router, you'll get better results when the work or the router is easier to control.

Sharpness and flute design are the essential elements that provide for efficiency and good control. Spirals are the most efficient, followed by on-shear and then straight. The number of flutes also plays a role, but two-fluted cutters dominate. Single-flute tools have balance problems, and three- or four-fluted bits (the least popular) sacrifice deflection resistance for cuts per inch. Spiral-ground bits have an advantage in both efficiency and wear. On-shear tools, with the edge at a slight angle, usually require a ¾-in. minimum diameter, so the majority of straight and other small-diameter bits are usually found without shear flutes. Decorative profile cutters are often shear-fluted, and they are plentiful.

Given the choice, I'd buy an on-shear tool over a straight perpendicular flute. The efficiencies are particularly noticeable in production, as the power demand will decrease with the on-shear tool. For the hobbyist who may only rout a few weekends a month, the difference may not be noticed. Heavy users, however, may get by with less horsepower because of the efficiency—and the cutter will run cooler and last longer.

Cutter Life

Some carbide bits last longer than others, but the difference is relatively small. There are too many variables to make a science out of testing the bits. The results from one type of test may not be significant for another type. For example, pathway cutting (cutting a tunnel) is at least twice as abusive on the same cutter as an edge cut.

Carbide bits are fairly equal, except that solid carbide lasts somewhat longer than carbide bits with welded or brazed cutting edges. (The carbide for solid carbide tools has been selected for hardness and durability, not braising, which compromises durability.)

Think about cutter life in terms of how it affects the work. If precision and cleanliness on a long run are essential, whether for joinery or decoration, I opt for two-stage cuts. I'll do 70 percent to 80 percent of the cut

Shaper cutters, which have holes for the arbor, cut the same profiles as router bits—such as the straight cutter at right—but will outlast them by a factor or 10 or more.

Close inspection reveals the cutter wear line on the work. The slight step will frustrate or prevent a close-fitting joint.

with one cutter and finish-cut the remaining 20 percent to 30 percent with a new tool at full depth in one pass. Uniform, light cuts may extend cutter life three to five times.

Your cutter is ready for a regrind when it starts burning stock, needs more hand-feed pressure and shows wear lines on the work. Joinery cutters (glue joint, rabbet, straight, or dovetail) used for extended periods at one depth will show wear lines at another depth. If you run 50 ft. of a ¼-in. by ¼-in. rabbet on MDF and then make a ⁵⁄₁₆-in.-square rabbet, the ¼-in. wear line will likely show up. For a decorative profile cut, the wear line may not matter; but for a dovetail and socket, the parts may not fit properly. Both cutters will still cut, but they are effectively dead soldiers.

Materials

Router bits vary in material. HSS used to be the cheapest and most commonly available. But most router bits for the small shop are now either carbide welded onto steel or solid carbide. Polycrystalline diamond is another option, but is used in production work only.

HIGH-SPEED STEEL
HSS is good material, and capable of very sharp edges that can be sharpened by the end user—but it doesn't hold up under prolonged use. With HSS, expect only 10 percent to 20 percent of the running time of carbide. Its value today is for the very short-run, custom profiles or perhaps for an experiment. If you're wondering about how the actual profile of a $35 carbide ogee might look, an $8 bit will give you the answer. And it might even serve for the short run in a given project.

Another advantage to HSS is that woodworkers skilled in tool grinding can make their own custom profiles. HSS router-bit blanks are available for this purpose. I especially like HSS bits for mortising, since they are often ground to plunge better than a carbide-faced steel bit, and a mortise run for a piece of furniture is usually a short run.

CARBIDE

Carbide on steel (the most common material and design) will outlast HSS 5 times to 10 times. Its actual life will vary, but it is clearly the best compromise for router-bit flutes, both economically and practically. The material can be reground (but never as well as the factory setup) sharp enough to run nearly as long. In my view, hand diamond honing is largely symbolic, and professionals should grind carbide for results and safety.

Carbide is the gold standard in tool-bit material today, although it does vary in hardness, durability, and density. Some carbide bits are selected for their durability in specific materials; one grade does not fit all occasions.

POLYCRYSTALLINE DIAMOND

Polycrystalline diamond (PCD) is very hard material, running 50 times to 100 times longer than carbide. This is strictly production material, mostly custom-made and designed to run for hours or days in materials like MDF, fiberglass, and aerospace composites. But cutters are very expensive, starting at about $200.

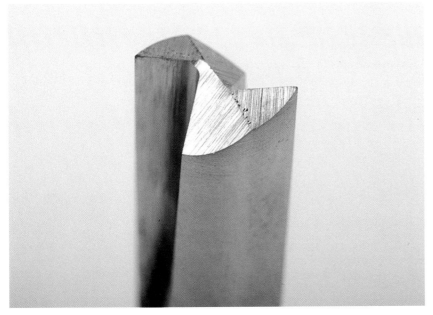

This Wisconsin Knife Works cutter has an over-center grind in the end of the flute for better plunging.

Shank Diameter

Shank diameters in the United States are ¼ in., ⁵⁄₁₆ in., ⅜ in., and ½ in.; metric sizes are common in Europe. Large shanks provide more surface area for the collet to surround, and also greater stiffness. Consequently, ½-in. shanks are the most popular. For a given tool geometry, there's often less machining required for a ½-in. tool than the ¼-in. equivalent. Consequently, they are about the same price. The advantage to smaller-shank tools is their small radii for closer inside cuts, or where it just makes no sense to use the larger shank. Trim routers use only ¼-in. shanks.

Cutter Types

There are many ways to classify router bits. They include piloted (with bearing) or unpiloted, bottom and side cutting, decorative profile, and joinery bits, as well as various combinations. Here's a sampling with special features you should know about.

BEARING BITS

The bearing used to guide a cutter can be placed on either end of the router bit or between a set of cutters, depending on the intended use. In all cases, they limit the cutting depth. Cutters with bearings on the end of the tool typically roll along the work and are often attached to decorative profile bits. Bevels, ogees, roundovers, coves, and beads are the typical cutters. They can be used in the hand router or on the router table. Essentially, they cut various profiles. These cutters are plentiful, cheap, competitive and probably the most popular of all router bits. They remove a lot of wood—and some (raised-panel bits) are enormous. Often, they are of anti-kickback design.

Solid carbide bits last longer than the same-sized bit with brazed-on carbide tips, left. Unfortunately, few cutters are solid carbide.

The Amana Nova Cutter System has replaceable carbide cutters that lock into the arbor assembly. Their carbide, not having to be brazed, has been selected for its keen edge.

Bearings come in a variety of sizes and can fit above, below, or between cutters.

The anti-kickback tool has a lot more steel in it than a conventional bit, and runs smoother because of its greater mass and even balance. The cutter design is such that it can only chop at the rate of 1 in. to $\frac{3}{64}$ in. per revolution. The gullets of these bits are shallow, and stock doesn't get caught in them; they don't kick back the work. I must add that the cut quality at 20,000 rpm is indistinguishable from that of a standard cutter at that speed—and that both will certainly cut you.

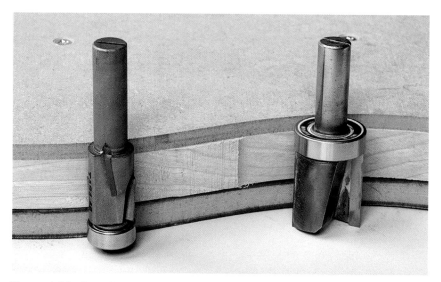

The sandwich of template-work-template shows two bearing and cutter options for the same result. The top-bearing pattern bit is easier to set up and there are more cutter options.

BEARING IN THE MIDDLE

A few bits have bearings sandwiched between two cutters top and bottom. The bearing maintains the space between the cutters and provides a means to limit the sideways depth of cut. It is strange that the most popular of these, the rail and stile sets, use a bearing at all. This is a router table tool only, and most door work is straight-line and should be worked off the fence. Nonetheless, these sets are supplied with bearings. Tongue-and-groove cutters and a few other miscellaneous bits are supplied with cutters or bearings sandwiched between each other.

BEARING ON THE TOP

Straight bits with a bearing mounted on the top are most often used with templates. They roll along the edge of a template for an exact transfer of the design to the workpiece. The practical and safe limit for full-thickness template cuts is about 1½ in. Longer cutters are common but should be avoided. You can, however, use incremental steps to reach deeper. If a 2-in.-thick piece of work, for example, is routed with a 1½-in. trimmer, you can use the machined surface of the stock to complete the cut. Essentially, all top-bearing tools are used with the template on top of the work. Using a template below the work requires a trimmer with a bearing on the end.

DECORATIVE PROFILE CUTTERS

Most cutters that decorate do so along the edges and ends of the work. They are important and occupy one-third to one-half or more of most cutter catalog inventories. These cutters usually have ball bearings to limit the depth of cut to about one radius. Moreover, the bearing-guided tools were designed primarily for the hand-held router. Ogees, bevels, beads, coves, and so on are generally supplied with R-3 bearings (O.D. = $\frac{1}{2}$ in., I.D.= $\frac{3}{16}$ in.). If the work is manageable and the cutter won't come apart, these profiles should be routed on the table without bearings. These cutters produce a lot of waste that can be easily collected, and the work is more efficient when guided off the table fence. There is also less operator risk than with the hand router.

For example, a 6-in.-diameter router (the typical base casting diameter) always has less than 50 percent of its footprint on the work while edge routing. If a 1$\frac{1}{2}$-in.-diameter ogee bit is in the router, then on startup there is only 38 percent of the router on the work—a hazard indeed. When the bearing (say an R-3) does finally engage the edge of the work, that number increases to 46 percent. But as the router turns the corner to rout the ends, less than 25 percent of the base is fully supported. This momentary instability is a big reason that burning and kickback are so likely at the ends of a workpiece. This doesn't happen on the router table.

BEARING ON THE BOTTOM

Flush-trim bits are designed to trim a workpiece to the size of the template or underlying substrate. These cutters are typically used with the hand router, but can just as easily be used on the router table. With a router table, more time and skill are required to make the template and safely fasten the template to the work. It is relatively easy to just clamp the template to the work on the bench and use the hand router.

A pattern bit, left, has to have its entire flute extended for the bearing to engage the template. The end-bearing flush-trim bit can be extended the minimum amount to engage its template.

Flush-trim bits are safer than top-bearing-guided tools because they do not "bottom cut," and you can always extend just enough bit to do the cutting. But with the shank-bearing tools, the whole flute has to be extended for the bearing to engage the template. Moreover, these tools (top-bearing cutters) are bottom cutters, and as such present another cutting surface where none is needed. The end bearing on the flush trimmer covers up the sharp edge at the end of the tool for additional safety.

Flush trimmers are very popular but due to the poor selection of standard bearings most are only ½ in. diameter with narrow webs of $\frac{7}{32}$ in. or less. What that means is increased deflection. No matter how sharp or who supplies them, these tools will deflect significantly when their flutes are an inch or longer. There just isn't sufficient metal left in the core of the tool to keep it from bending. The few ¾-in. cutting diameter (½-in. shank) flush trimmers are very strong, however.

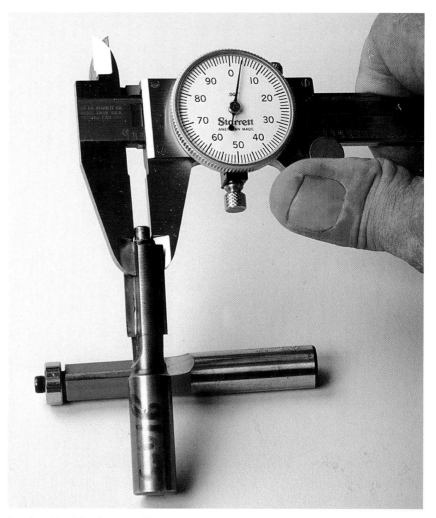

In spite of its ½-in. diameter, this trimmer is pretty narrow in the web, less than ¼ in. at the end of the tool.

Bits for interlocking joinery must meet high grinding standards to do their job. Your setup must also be exact to minimize errors.

Though the faces of this glue joint don't line up, the profiles do nest in one another.

JOINERY BITS

Routers are good at joinery. Common joints include half lap, tongue and groove, mortise and tenon, cope and stick, scarf, finger, glue, and dovetail. Many cutters are precision-ground precisely for the job; others are not. Some dovetail bits are job-specific; so are the glue joint and cope-and-stick cutters. Half-lap, tongue-and-groove, and mortise-and-tenon bits are nonspecific but require precision nonetheless. For the most part, good joinery is quite dependent on good milling and good jigs and fixtures—and less on

Interchangeable cutters used on a separate arbor provide an alternative to individual bits with arbors.

the cutter itself. Nevertheless, it can be very frustrating to discover that a poor fit is caused by the cutter.

As a matter of routine, I make a practical check on the fit of a sample joint before I commit the cutters to joinery on real project sticks. Direct cutter measurement may not reveal the potential for error, and certain cutters require sophisticated measuring tools and a good understanding of trigonometry and geometry to predict their behavior. It is easier and more important to actually test a cutter on scrap. If you don't, you'll risk spoiling expensive stock.

MULTIPIECE BITS

Most manufacturers of router bits make a few cutters that are assembled onto an arbor. Sometimes it's done out of necessity for the speed of production. It might just be cheaper to make the cutter than grind the whole thing out of one chunk of metal. Sometimes it's done to give the user a choice, say an $\frac{1}{8}$-in. vs. a $\frac{1}{4}$-in. slot cutter. Sometimes it's done for the sake of economy.

Expect a little more vibration with multipiece cutters and pay attention to the assembly directions. A cutter accidentally placed upside down can burn out in a minute, or break.

Examples of scary, potentially dangerous bits, from left: The 10-oz. lock miter's diameter is 5½ times larger than its shank. The rabbet bit is five times greater. The big dovetail bit has less than a ³⁄₁₆ in. of steel in the web. The HSS spiral bit is so flexible it "zings" when it cuts. And the carbide O-flute is 12 times longer than its diameter.

Sharpening

All cutting tools get dull. As they lose their cutting edge, their power demand to cut increases, the tools are worked harder and dulling increases at a faster and faster rate. A router bit's life is short, so I have developed strategies to increase it. One way to increase cutter life is to sequence its use. A cutter that burns in end grain, for example, may be acceptable on long grain; a cutter that won't cut edge grain will burn the end grain, but you can probably rout MDF with it. If it won't cut MDF, it may cut plastic but not for long. A cutter that won't cut plastic may abrade MDF but won't really slice it. To be sure, for the best of cuts on any material, use a new cutter.

Carbide grinding requires sophisticated diamond tooling; the stuff is hard. You can diamond hone it a little and you can sharpen high-speed steel. But to get the maximum time between sharpenings, expect to have your tools professionally ground. It is very cost-effective. Four to six regrinds are possible if the cutter has incurred no serious fractures. It is important to note that if 80 percent of the cutter life (if reground four times) is from the grinding service, not the manufacturer, finding a good grinder may be more important than finding a good manufacturer.

Router Accessories

A s mentioned, routers can't do much without a guide of some sort. A cutter without a bearing on it will require a router table or an accessory to control its pathway. Even cutters with bearings often require a jig or template to guide the tool around. It so happens there are quite a few accessories for routers—some that are manufactured and some that you can easily make yourself. Here's a sampling.

Guides and Bases

The collar guide is available from the manufacturer for most routers, whether fixed-base, plunge, or trim. These devices fasten to the subbase or the base casting, surround the cutter, and with the cutter act like a pattern bit, but with an offset between bit and guide. They are used with templates, especially with dovetail and joinery jigs. The router is pulled against the template to establish contact with the collar. The collar slides along the template and cuts a swath parallel or concentric to the pattern. A 1-in.-diameter tool bit is about the largest cutter that can be used with a collar.

INLAY KITS
Inlay kits include a collar, sleeve, and ⅛-in.-diameter cutter. The sleeve will offset the cutter pathway to compensate for diameter differences of the cutter and collar. If the cutter was like a laser and could cut with no waste, the plug and the recess it fits into could be created without the sleeve on the collar.

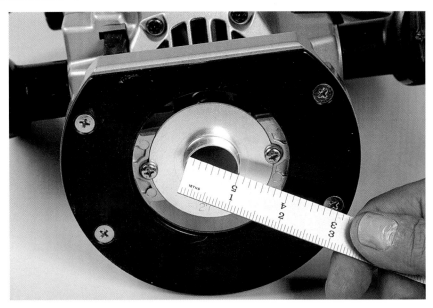

Collar guides that fit the opening in the router's baseplate allow the router to follow templates and other cutting jigs. The largest practical cutter diameter that can pass through most collars is 1 in.

Inlay kits use a pair of matched collar guides so you can follow the same pattern for both the excavation and the insert. The sizes are designed to compensate for the diameter of the bit.

Don't expect to do anything more than shallow decorative inlay work with these systems. The cutter is only a ⅛ in. in diameter—which is very short and not capable of deep or wide work. Note that you'll need to make pattern templates for most work with these kits.

With an aftermarket offset subbase and a shop-made edge guide, it's nearly impossible to spoil this decorative cut.

EDGE GUIDES

Edge guides fasten to the router-base casting with a pair of rods. Nearly all routers are designed to accept them, though not all manufacturers make them for their routers. The guides provide a means to cut parallel to the edge of the work. They are continuously adjustable and generally used with pilotless cutters. Add-on or replacement fences can be made concentric to inside or outside radii so the whole package (edge guide, router, and bit) can travel along curved edges.

ROUTER SUBBASES

Round, offset, square, and other shapes of subbases are available for transparency, control, and specialty application. Sears, DeWalt, Porter-Cable, Woodhaven, Vermont American, and others compete in this aftermarket niche (see Resources on p. 180).

CIRCLE CUTTING AND ELLIPSE MAKERS

Plastic pivot subbases are in most catalogs and the all steel and aluminum Micro Fence jig can cut precision circles (shown at right). The jig is also designed to work with an ellipse base, shown at far right, which provides an easy way to adjust the minor and major axes.

OLDER ORIGINAL EQUIPMENT ROUTER COLLETS often would let their cutters slip, or "glue," themselves to the cutter. Two wrenches, frequently different, were and still are a necessity for cutter exchanges. Newer collets are fastened to their collet nuts, rarely slip, and always free themselves from the bit. Still, there are those who think that is not enough.

Two aftermarket companies have been trying to create a market for wrenchless collets. The Jacobs Power Collet is toolless and the Eliminator chuck uses only a T-handled hex-key. They are somewhat router-specific, but given sufficient distribution, they should be available for all routers soon. They are bigger than the original collets and hold their cutters well, but they can vibrate more.

The Jacobs Power Collet replaces wrenches with a snap-in system that releases and tightens with a click.

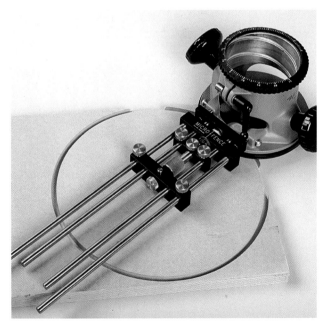

Micro Fence's adjustable circle cutting jig fits most routers and can be tuned to within a few thousandths of an inch.

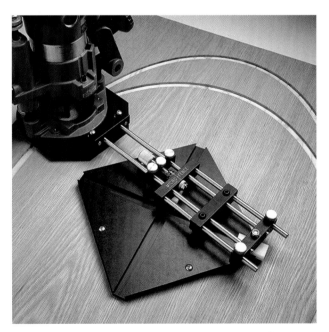

Used with an aftermarket jig, the Micro Fence can be used to rout precise ellipses. The mounting plate and a set of pivoting blocks provide a way to quickly set the minor and major axes of the ellipse.

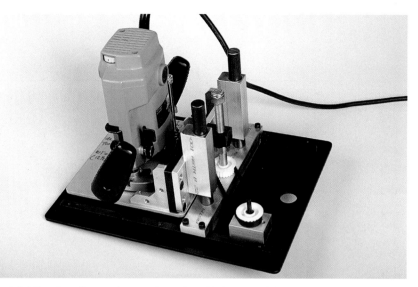

Rout-R-Lift, a Canadian product, replaces the table insert and cutter height adjustment with one product. A removable crank raises and lowers the router with a screw drive from the top of the table.

The DeWalt 621 plunge router has an accessory adjustment knob for fine adjustments—useful whether the router is upside down or right side up.

Rout-R-Lift top view.

Lee Valley's Router Bit Jack is attached to the depth stop of a plunge router. The tool allows depth changes with a lever. (Photo courtesy Lee Valley.)

Router Table Accessories

Routers are essentially designed for hand use and as such do not necessarily adjust up and down very well against gravity when underneath a router table. Extracting the springs from plunge routers and retrofitting the router with an aftermarket fine-depth adjuster are common strategies that can help.

A couple of different devices from Lee Valley and Jessem Tool Companies accomplish the same thing. The Jessem Rout-R-Lift is a substitute router table insert that carries the router in a crank-driven mechanism. The Lee Valley Router Bit Jack uses a ratchet mechanism fastened to a threaded rod of an upside-down plunger.

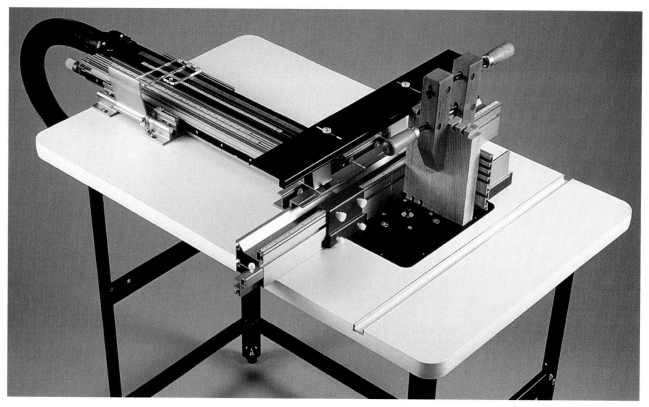

The router table fence from Incra Jig can be used as a standard fence and, with an attachment, for cutting dovetails. (Photo courtesy Incra Jig.)

ROUTER TABLE FENCES

Incra and JoinTech are the key players in aftermarket router table fences. The Incra Jig fence system moves a notch at a time on a saw-tooth rack, with a knob for fine adjustments between stops. The JoinTech uses a screw for continuous adjustment throughout its range. (See p. 91 for more on fences.)

PIN ROUTING

Pin routing is an interesting template method of routing whereby an overhead pin, in line with the cutter, engages the edge of the template fastened to the work. The cutter then trims the work even with or parallel to the template. Inside work is also possible with the system.

DOVETAIL/BOX-JOINT MAKERS

There are at least five dovetail jigs for hand routers; three of the five are capable of box, finger, and other case-corner joints. The Omni Jig is a Porter-Cable tool with many templates for box, through, half-blind, and sliding dovetails.

The JoinTech fence adjusts continuously and can be used on other stationary tools. (Photo courtesy JoinTech.)

The Porter-Cable Omni Jig is an industrial dovetail jig that has many accessories for various kinds of dovetails, as well as other joinery. (Photo courtesy Porter-Cable.)

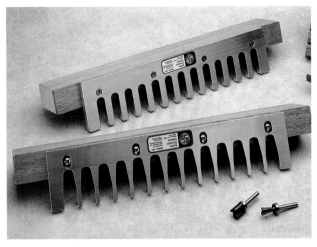

The Keller Dovetail System uses matched templates to cut precisely through dovetails on fixed centers. The idea is to do only through dovetails, but do them well and with a minimum of setup. (Photo courtesy Keller & Co.)

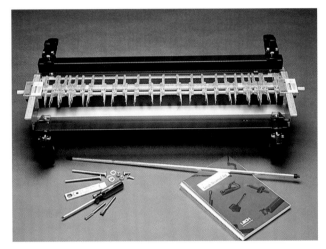

The Leigh Jig uses adjustable fingers for cutting variable-spaced dovetails, and it has become the industry standard for this operation. Leigh offers a wide variety of accessories for other joinery applications as well. (Photo courtesy Leigh Jig.)

Half-blind dovetail jigs—Porter-Cable 4112 is shown—are commonly used for drawer construction. The setup is rather fussy, though, and can require several test cuts. (Photo courtesy Porter-Cable.)

The Keller jig is a set of templates that clamp to the work, one for tails and the other for sockets or pins. The openings in the aluminum templates are fixed so the dovetails are cut on fixed centers.

Leigh Jig is the most versatile of the joint makers, capable of variable-spaced dovetails, box joints, and decorative interlocking joints shaped like flowers. The work is clamped to the bench-supported jig.

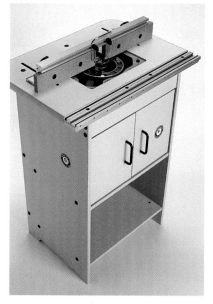

This router table from Bench Dog comes with an adjustable split fence system and built-in tracks for accessories. (Photo courtesy Bench Dog.)

Many routers are now being fitted with chip-collection tubes. From left: DeWalt 621, DeWalt 625, and Porter-Cable 7529.

This over-arm pin router assembly is used with a template attached to the top of the workpiece. It's very efficient for making multiples of pieces with a complex shape. It's also capable of inside template routing. (Photo courtesy Lee Valley.)

The Katie Jig and the Stotts Template Making Jig also compete in the fixed-space, through-dovetail jigs for hand routers.

Finally, there are a number of half-blind dovetail makers by Porter-Cable, Sears, and many others. These are for making drawers in varying widths.

Chip Collection

Routers make a lot of waste. At 300 cuts to 400 cuts per second, they can only produce wafer-thin chips. These should be collected as soon as possible for your health and the quality of the cut. The DeWalt 625 has an aftermarket vacuum funnel accessory, as does the Porter-Cable router system. Router tables, the biggest chip producers, should all have a vacuum system.

A router table is a necessity rather than an accessory for many woodworkers. There are at least 16 choices, varying in size, material, design, and price. Prices with both accessories and router can run up to $500 or more. See chapter 6 for more on router tables.

Simple Shopmade Jigs

Shopmade router jigs and fixtures use the router to its limits. These jigs and fixtures can be very simple or extremely complex. Some of the fixtures I've seen are so sophisticated that you'd need to be a machinist to build them.

Router jigs and fixtures essentially serve to hold and index the work, as well as provide a guide for a controlled cut. At times, the jig or fixture holds the work so the cutting can be done on the router table. At other times, they hold the work so a handheld router can be used easily and safely. Either way, jigs and fixtures can be thought of as safety devices for precise, manageable and controlled routing.

Right-Angle Templates

Right-angle templates are similar to bench hooks used as holders and cutting guides with hand tools. Used with clamps, they hold the work and establish a pathway for the router to cut perpendicular to the edge of the work. Use them with collar guides or pattern bits.

I make mine from ½-in. MDF. The template should be at least as long as the work is wide and 6 in. to 8 in. wide. Two or three different lengths are better than one size for all. Screw and glue a 1x2-in. cleat to the bottom of the template. To get the most out of one of these, square both working edges to the front edge of the cleat.

Right-angle bench hooks register off the front edge of the work. They can be used with a collar guide, as shown. Backup scrap is clamped to the rear of the template to prevent tearout and breakout.

The adjustable stop on my fence is useful for cuts like open mortises.

Slot Makers

Adjustable stops with slotted ways are quite common in woodworking, but without a jig they're not easy to make. I solve this problem by creating a window slot template. I clamp the work under the template and use a collar guide and plunge router to make the slot. The width of the slot is usually one cutter diameter, and its length is regulated with the stop.

Make the platform from ½-in. MDF and big enough to clamp to the work—about 11 in. by 17 in. Make the narrow opening just wide enough

Slotted mortises require a jig. Here, the workpiece fits underneath, and the pattern bit runs in the slot.

for your collar to slip in—1 in. is a common collar diameter. Make the slot longer than the longest slot you plan to use—6 in. in my case.

You'll need some fences underneath to register the work, and on which to mount a clamp. Slot the MDF fences for a pair of screws and washers so they are easy to adjust.

Shopmade Mortiser

A good mortise is essential to quality joinery. There are many ways to make them, each with its advantages and limitations. Given well-milled material, a good plunge router, two edge guides, and my shop-built mortiser (see the top photo on p. 134), I can index and excavate a mortise up to $2\frac{3}{8}$ in. deep in just a minute or so.

A block of straight-grained hardwood is the foundation of the jig. Make it about $1\frac{1}{4}$ in. by $4\frac{1}{2}$ in. by 24 in. and screw on some $1\frac{1}{2}$-in. by $1\frac{1}{2}$-in. stock of the same species for more router surface. Add a cleat to the bottom of each side—one for jackscrews to support the work, and the other as a hold-down.

A set of three toggle clamps screwed to one of the cleats will secure and index the work. To be sure, a pair of adjustable stops on the top of the jig will simplify the mortising process. Position and slot them for the lengths of mortises you expect to make. A big, flat washer and machine screw will hold them in place.

This mortising jig uses a pair of sliding rods so it can easily adjust to make many mortise widths.

This simple tenoning jig uses a rabbeting bit with a ball bearing and an oversized router base to cut square tenons. The plunge mechanism allows you to cut a deeper tenon than the width of the rabbeting bit.

Tenon Maker

Square shouldered, clean-faced straight tenons are a snap with my shop-made tenoner (above). The windowed platform, combined with a plunge router on a wide wood base, are the key components to routing precise tenons. The work is indexed, clamped, and squared up from below, and the long-shank rabbet bit makes the tenon cheeks from above. Shoulder widths vary as the diameter of the bit and bearing differ.

For the body of the jig, use ¾-in. MDF or maple. Screws, dadoes, and angle brackets are used for the assembly. Cut a window in the top for work and cutter access. Also cut one in the vertical member so the cutter can access the entire section of the work.

You can clamp the jig to the bench when routing short stock, or clamp the work in a vise with the jig clamped to the work for big and long sticks.

An adjustable fence that pivots will permit angled tenons. A small toggle clamp on the fence will facilitate setup, but at least one other C-clamp will be needed to hold the work safely.

Tenon Maker

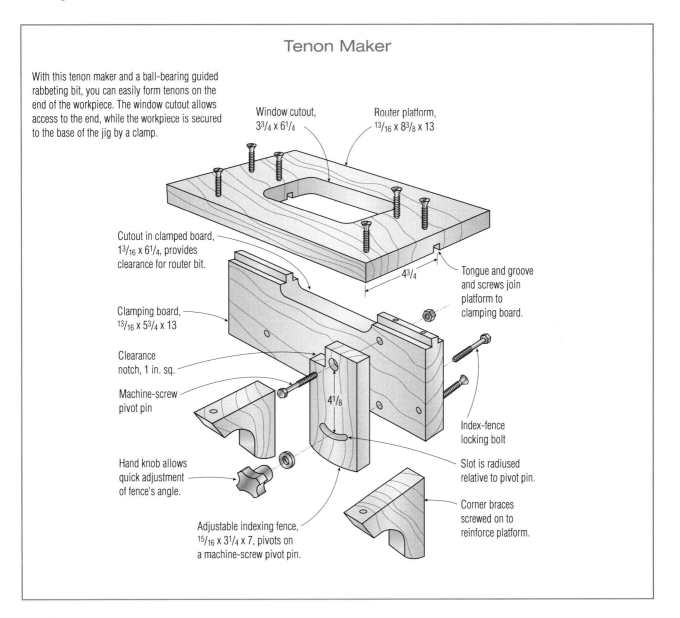

With this tenon maker and a ball-bearing guided rabbeting bit, you can easily form tenons on the end of the workpiece. The window cutout allows access to the end, while the workpiece is secured to the base of the jig by a clamp.

Window cutout, 3³/₄ x 6¹/₄

Router platform, ¹³/₁₆ x 8³/₈ x 13

Cutout in clamped board, 1¹³/₁₆ x 6¹/₄, provides clearance for router bit.

4³/₄

Tongue and groove and screws join platform to clamping board.

Clamping board, ¹³/₁₆ x 5³/₄ x 13

Clearance notch, 1 in. sq.

Machine-screw pivot pin

4¹/₈

Index-fence locking bolt

Hand knob allows quick adjustment of fence's angle.

Slot is radiused relative to pivot pin.

Corner braces screwed on to reinforce platform.

Adjustable indexing fence, ¹⁵/₁₆ x 3¹/₄ x 7, pivots on a machine-screw pivot pin.

Shown is the underside of a half-lap jig. The workpiece is clamped in place and the router excavates the lap through the window.

End-Lap Template

End laps are simple enough visually, but hard to cut precisely. The shoulder must be square and the face must be equal to the mate it overlays. The lap is usually cut to half its thickness. A pattern bit and template are about all you need. The work is clamped under the template and exposed to the cutter through the window. A right-angle fence squares the work to the critical edge of the template. I use a large subbase on the router to keep it from tipping into the window.

Since lap cuts are so shallow, this jig can be made from ⅝-in.- or ¾-in.-thick MDF. This template and its construction are similar to the tenon jig—only this time, the work edge of the window must be at a right angle to the fence.

Make the jig big enough to clamp to the bench. Hold the work with toggle clamps fastened to the fence. A cleat fastened just beyond the window with a screw through it can serve as an adjustable stop. The end of the workpiece is butted against the screw, but below the work's thickness centerline to prevent an encounter with the router bit. If you work on both faces of the stock, you can make two-faced tenons.

Adjustable Tenon Maker

Dovetail and straight tenons are made with a fixed or plunge router using bearings or collars. The work has to be reversed and cut equally from both sides to yield centered tenons. The straight template is coupled to a screw and rotating lever for continuous adjustment. The work is clamped to the fixture, which is clamped to the bench/beam.

Make this one out of wood, aluminum, and MDF for the adjustable template. Make a right-angle assembly as long as the widest stock you plan to work, plus 8 in. or so for a fence, a clamp pedestal, and a hold-fast. You must be able to fix the jig to a rigid structure.

The template should be 5 in. or wider for plenty of router support. It travels on a set of 1-in. parallel bars mortised into the platform and the

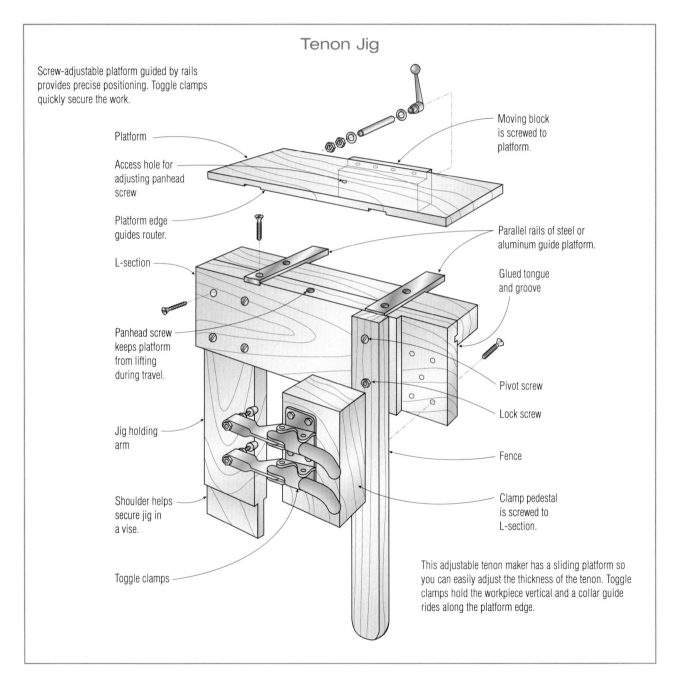

Tenon Jig

Screw-adjustable platform guided by rails provides precise positioning. Toggle clamps quickly secure the work.

Platform

Access hole for adjusting panhead screw

Platform edge guides router.

L-section

Panhead screw keeps platform from lifting during travel.

Jig holding arm

Shoulder helps secure jig in a vise.

Toggle clamps

Moving block is screwed to platform.

Parallel rails of steel or aluminum guide platform.

Glued tongue and groove

Pivot screw

Lock screw

Fence

Clamp pedestal is screwed to L-section.

This adjustable tenon maker has a sliding platform so you can easily adjust the thickness of the tenon. Toggle clamps hold the workpiece vertical and a collar guide rides along the platform edge.

This adjustable tenon jig is used with collar guides to cut precise tenons. One turn of the lever is 0.055 in. of template travel.

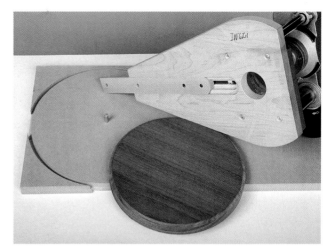

A homemade circle jig can be easily made up from hardwood scrap. An adjustable slide rides in a groove and pivots on a pin.

A router horse elevates the work and is more convenient than a router table for many operations.

template itself. It is driven by a screw that is $\frac{5}{16}$ in. in diameter by 18 threads per inch.

Two clamps on the pedestal secure the work. A fence (pivoting a few degrees) squares the work to the template. The hold-fast is 4 in. wide and screwed and rabbeted to the jig.

Circle Maker

This subbase (above) has a sliding pivot stick to make circles or disks. Use it with a plunge router and a solid carbide straight bit for best results.

The shape of the tool is not critical, but should be as small as practical. The bigger it gets, the more likely it is to bang into clamps as it revolves. You could also use a paddle with holes in it, but a jig with a fully adjustable arm is a lot handier.

Make the jig from $\frac{5}{8}$-in. maple with a long slot in it for an adjustable slide. If you want, make several slides of different lengths for convenience. Put a few holes in the slide for a pivot pin. A flat-head machine screw enters the bottom of the slide, and extends through the slot and into a nut on top to secure the arm.

Router Horse

Most hand-routed work is either done on an assembly or a loose stick. Assemblies are usually stable enough to rout clamped to the bench without much ado. Sticks, on the other hand, could use a lift. This short beam, shown at left, was made with lots of overhang to get the work up high enough to rout comfortably. Normal 34-in.- to 36-in.-high assembly benches are too low to rout on.

Router Horse

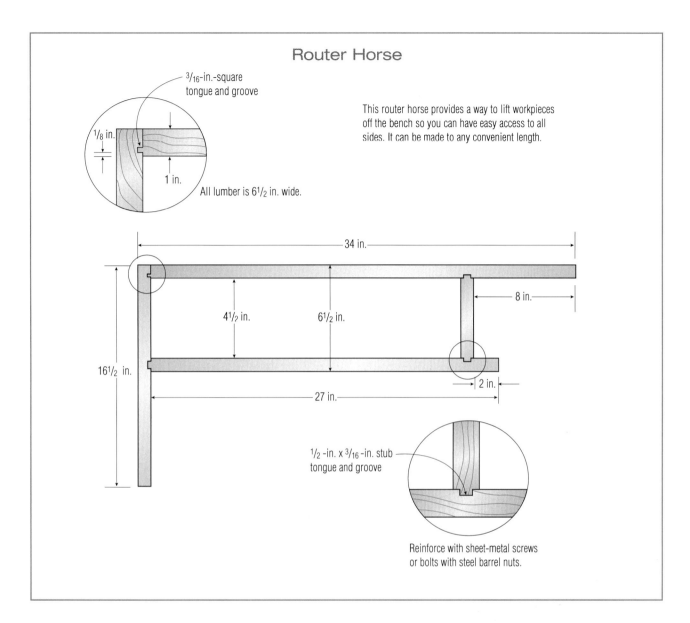

3/16-in.-square
tongue and groove

1/8 in.

1 in.

All lumber is 6½ in. wide.

This router horse provides a way to lift workpieces off the bench so you can have easy access to all sides. It can be made to any convenient length.

34 in.

8 in.

4½ in.

6½ in.

16½ in.

27 in.

2 in.

½ -in. x 3/16 -in. stub
tongue and groove

Reinforce with sheet-metal screws
or bolts with steel barrel nuts.

Make this 1-in.-thick jig about 6 in. high and 36 in. long. A 6-in. to 8-in. width will support a 10-in.- to 12-in.-wide workpiece. The tool is joined in four places. The overhang on the horizontal surface is somewhat arbitrary: allow about 4 in. to 8 in. The vertical end piece is overhung by 10 in. to allow better support for workpieces held on end.

There is no need to complicate this; just hold the jig together with shallow dadoes and a little hardware. The bottom stick is used to hold the jig down and is pinned by a clamp. After assembly, add a fence to the vertical panel and again, some handy toggle clamps to hold the work on end. The right-angle jig can be used to advantage here, for making tenons or dadoes.

Permanent C-Clamps

A clamp with a welded-on plate can permanently attach a deep C-clamp to a jig. With a clamp screwed down through the steel plate, a jig becomes a sturdy platform that can support beefy workpieces, so all sorts of routing can be done from many directions.

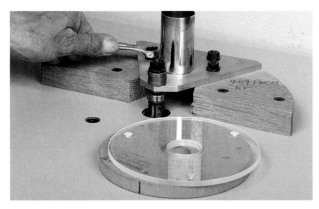

The shop made pin router jig will allow you to easily make multiples of complex shapes. The template goes on top and rolls against the pin.

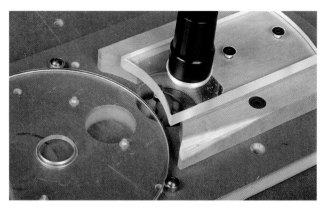

This jig is used to cut bevels on the edges of round stock. The work rolls on the two bearings and the cutter is exposed through the cutter window.

Pin-Routing Jig

Pin routing is essentially a router table operation. A bearing or pin is suspended above or hung below and in line with the cutter. A template and work sandwich is rolled along the bearing, which follows the template contour and transfers that to the workpiece. The system is nearly the same as routing with end bearings, but in this case the isolated pin (or idler bearing) gets all the sideways stress, and thus the cuts are cleaner. As a rule, the pin router is a production tool.

You needn't make the jig quite this fancy (above left), but these are production tools. Mine is cut from a 1-in.-thick by 12-in. oak semicircle. Use thicker material if you plan on routing more than ¾-in.-thick stock. Add an equal share to the thickness of the jig for additional work thickness. Cut a notch in the front for a chip pocket. A vacuum tube on top of the jig collects the chips.

I used aluminum plate for mounting the pilot bearing. A ¼-in. shoulder bolt secures the bearing to the plate. The plate's screw holes are ⁹⁄₃₂ in., and the screws that go through these holes are ¼ in.

45-Degree Bevel

On occasion, I'll make a run of round replacement subbases. The two bearings ensure the disk has two points to roll on. I raise or lower the cutter to adjust the depth of cut.

I made this tool (above right) from ¾-in. MDF. The bearings can be situated in three places for different-sized disks. The small wooden platform, also screwed to the jig, is for a vacuum tool holder. The sub assembly also makes it harder to get my fingers near the cutter. The jig gets bolted down to the router table; its position is not critical. The base is 9 in. by 15 in., but size isn't important. Be sure to make it big enough if you're clamping it to the table.

Alignment Aid

To center and align a pin-router bearing, use a ¼-in. pilot pin installed in the router collet. The pin is available from most woodworking supply houses and is simply a machined piece of steel used for alignment chores. Simply project the pilot pin through the hole for the shoulder bolt in the aluminum plate—then tighten the screws down on the plate. Remove the pilot pin and install the ¼-in. bolt and bearing.

Router Safety

Compared to other technologies, woodworking and machinery processes change slowly. The hazards and risks associated with power and hand tools are essentially the same as they were decades ago. It's a dangerous business and accidents are common—a fact that's reflected by insurance rates for woodworkers.

Working with wood requires sharp cutting tools often used very close to the operator's body. It should come as no surprise that butchers use bandsaws on animal carcasses, and orthopedic surgeons use hammers, chisels, circular saws, drills, knives, and sanders on humans.

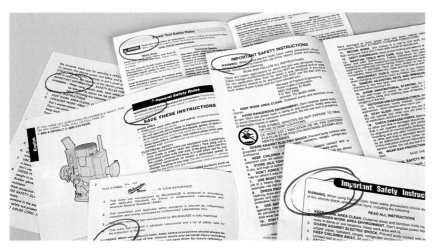

The rules of router safety are similar from manual to manual, but it's still a good idea to read them.

Hearing protection and a dust mask are sensible precautions.

Woodworking machinery is in the dark ages compared to the automobile, as far as safety goes. The automobile industry has done a thorough job in protecting drivers while in the cars they are driving and from the ones they may crash into. Seat restraints, air bags, hazard lights, ABS brakes, door panel guards, telescoping steering columns, safety glass, and padded dashboards all protect the driver. However, defensive driving skills are still as important as ever. In woodworking as well, it's just as important to play an active role in your own safety, to learn how to prevent accidents and to practice that skill constantly.

I make it a point to read all router safety rules in texts, articles, and router owners' manuals. These manuals are very poor; but you should read them nevertheless, because in this book, I am going to omit information on routing in an electrical storm, wearing OSHA-approved safety glasses, and the regulations on jewelry, long hair, long sleeves, and long extension cords. I am also not going to repeat the material on overreach, children in proximity, operator fatigue, the influence of alcohol or drugs, forcing the tool, good housekeeping, or saving instructions for future use. I will tell you about the things that have scared me, nearly injured me, and taken me by surprise. These experiences have led me to develop some precautions that you won't find in the operator's manual.

I should point out that all of my accidents and near-accidents were entirely my fault. I've never had an accident due to equipment failure. I've wrecked an acre of wood, but I've never drawn blood from a broken tool or a machine failure. And as we all know, there are general health issues besides the direct physical dangers of routing.

Hand-Router Safety

Fixed-base and plunge routers were first designed for upright use in the hands of the woodworker—not to be inverted under a router table. If they are used within their design limits, they are pretty safe. They are intimidating and scary, but they are safe.

CUTTING RESISTANCE

The amount of cutter engaged in the work determines its "grip" in the stock. Cutter traction increases roughly by the square. In other words, the area swept out in a ⅜-in. by ⅜-in. cut is nine times greater than a ⅛-in. by ⅛-in. rabbet, not three times. As such, the cutting dynamics are somewhat

The cutting procedure for the ⅛-in. by ⅛-in. rabbet, left, is the same for the ⅜-in. by ⅜-in. rabbet, right, but the volume swept out in the latter is nine times greater than the smaller cut. Expect substantial changes in handling as you scale up.

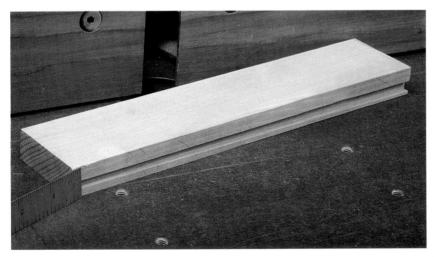

Neglect the motor lock in the router table and expect the depth of cut to change like it did while routing this slot.

unpredictable. Don't expect the same control when doubling the cut. If you're in doubt, make depth changes in small increments. The differences are especially noticeable in end grain where the fibers are at right angles to the cutting direction. Expect more exertion on end-grain or cross-grain cuts like dadoes.

SPONTANEOUS DEPTH CHANGES

On occasion, a motor may spontaneously shift in the casting, or a cutter may loosen in the collet. A plunge motor may also move on its posts if it's not tightened down enough. The consequences can range from a minor mishap to ruined work.

It is your responsibility to make sure the motor in a fixed-base tool does not move under power. They rarely do, but I believe wing-nut lock levers should be replaced with longer levers for more tightening purchase. Plunge levers should also be positioned so they don't run out of twist-travel before locking up the motor. All plunge lock levers have an adjustment for this.

INSTABILITY

Routers can unexpectedly tip when under power. They can be awkward to use and difficult to hold securely as you work. Fixed-base tools are sometimes used on narrow edges, or with less than half their baseplates on the work. In either case, a bobble can cause the cutter to dig into the work, even breaking or bending the cutter and resulting in kickback. Often, the router table is a better choice for narrow stock because it allows much better control. You can also use offset router bases, as shown below, that allow for more control by making it easier to press down directly over the workpiece. In this case, even an oversized subbase can make a big difference.

The locking lever of this Porter-Cable 690 router has been replaced with a longer version. The extra length provides more torque for easier locking.

Adding an oversized subbase to a plunge router, shown at lower left, can add a lot of stability to the tool.

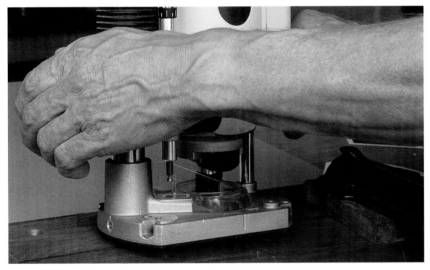

The cutter is loosely trapped between two sticks of equal thickness, set to the maximum intended depth for the cut. Test with a 5-lb. or 10-lb. push to see if the tool is unstable.

A plunge router under similar conditions can also tip. The handles are widely spaced and often high up on the posts. If a long cutter is engaged in a deep cut, your hand-feed forces may tip the tool over.

VARIABLE SPEED AND SOFT START

Variable speed is a relatively new feature in routers and a good one—especially for slowing down large-diameter cutters. Also, all variable speed tools have soft (ramp) start, a nice safety feature. Nevertheless, slow-speed routing can be risky. At slower speeds, cutting efficiency is reduced and it

---

Dry Run to Test Setup

Even though you won't be cutting stock, it's a good idea to get the feel of a plunge cut before you start the motor. Simulate the cut with the motor off and the cutter at its maximum depth. Move the router along to get the feel of it and to make sure the operation will go easily and smoothly. For difficult cuts, it's always a good idea to do a test cut in scrap stock.

takes more hand-feed force to move the work or router. As a result, the risk for up-ending the router increases and adequate clamping is essential. Before routing at slow speed, push and pull on the work, fences, stops, and edge guides to check their security: you'll be using more force than usual.

If you do start a cutter spinning and engage it in the work before it reaches maximum cutting speed, you may break or bend it. A soft-start tool has little rotational kinetic kickback on startup, so the likelihood of the cutter slamming into something before it is at maximum rpm is less of a problem. Consider a soft-start variable-speed tool to be the equivalent of a shock absorber in your car, thus making accidents such as bit grabbing in end grain less terrifying. Without this feature, the kinetics (reaction forces) during cutter jams and bobble are spontaneous and much more frightening.

Aftermarket Speed Controls

CLAIMS ARE MADE THAT AFTERMARKET SPEED CONTROLS are as good as the variable-speed feedback microprocessors in new routers. In my view, that is not true, and some toolmakers will not guarantee their tools with aftermarket devices in use.

Variable-speed controls on routers are not particularly accessible—and for good reason. Speed-control devices are used to slow down large-diameter tools; at high speeds they present more risk. If the speed control is very accessible, it could accelerate with an accidental bump, thus causing an accident.

In any case, if you use one of these, protect it from an accidental dial change. Early advertisements showed the contraption on the operator's belt—a very unsafe practice.

Big cutters require larger clearance holes than is necessary for most operations. A spare MDF fence can solve the problem.

With this template on a slight incline, you can rout a grip into the side of this box.

Incorporating a switch in the outside of a router table base provides safety insurance by allowing for quick shut-off in the case of an emergency. The switch is mortised so it can't be accidently struck.

KEEPING THE ROUTER HORIZONTAL

There will be occasions when routing with the router sideways (spindle horizontal) may look like a tempting solution to your woodworking problem. I would resist that temptation. Not only will you get chips in your face and hair, but the dynamics of the operation are so peculiar that it is invariably dangerous. Routing on an angle, however, is safe as long as the angle is not steep enough to make the router easily tip.

Router Table Safety

As a router table woodworker, you should keep a few things uppermost in your mind. Most basic of all is keeping the router secure in its casting while mounted upside down in the table. Failure to tighten the clamps can also have obvious drastic consequences. And clearly, your router table must be secured while you work. Also key is wiring a switch into your router table so that you can quickly turn it off.

With these basic precautions, the router table is pretty safe most of the time, but there are some risks. In general, you should use a split fence for safety's sake. You can more easily true up fence halves and slide the halves left and right to crowd the cutter, thus exposing the minimum steel. Vacuum collection and a solid means of securing the fence are essential. Without a secure fence, a slip could make the router grab the work, or you could lose your balance.

This pair of 2½-in.-long levers, at 6 in. from either end of the fence, securely lock the fence in place. The levers lock into T-nuts under the table.

Don't do this. Sliding the work down the fence onto this spinning cutter is done at considerable risk. If the fence moves, you can lose your grip on the work; or if the work is bowed you can break the cutter.

SMALL WORK

Work that is too small for the hand router can be table routed, but a great table and fence are not reason enough to get your hands close to the cutter. Avoid unnecessary reliance on hold-ins and hold-downs whenever possible. They obscure the cutter and hinder control of the workpiece. If the work seems hazardous enough to use hold-downs, it should be the signal that another kind of jig or fixture is required. You'll need a fixture big enough to keep your hands away from the cutter and sturdy enough to serve as a platform for stops and clamps. The jig may not be easy or quick to make, but your results will be better—and much cheaper than an emergency room visit.

DOUBLE-BLIND ENDED TABLE CUTS

Dropping the work on a spinning cutter is dangerous. It is a common but risky practice. Selecting the end points of the cut is guesswork, changing depth for mortises (and other cuts) is difficult, and handling the work is precarious. Any relaxation or momentary loss of control is "curtains." Expect chattered walls and burns at the ends of the piece as you reverse direction. You'll kill the cutter prematurely, and this is an unsafe practice. The hand plunge router was invented to accommodate these blind cuts, so you should use it.

THE HIDDEN CUTTER

It's common when working on a router table to have the cutter buried much of the time during a cut, only to have it appear unexpectedly at the end. It's important to stay alert; you must play an active part in your own safety. The sudden appearance of the cutter is just as threatening as a cutter that is always in your face.

ROUTING CURVY WORK

For routing on a curve, the usual strategy is to use bearing-guided cutters with a starting pin off to the side so you can ease the workpiece into the spinning cutter. Without one, the work is likely to kick away from the cutter. Even with a pin, it's possible that the cutter will catch the starting corner and whisk the work out of your control. Whenever possible, add a little sacrificial material to the end of the work for an easier start. In any case, you should feed the material against the cutter rotation.

Making the groove is so effortless, one may forget there is a cutter soon to emerge as the work passes over it.

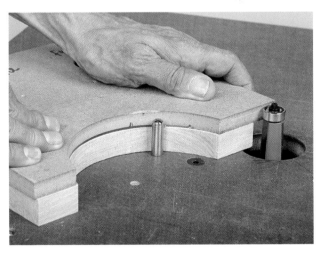

A starting pin allows you to start the work in a controlled way—a safety essential with curved work.

Cuts that run around the entire workpiece can begin anywhere, but it is safer to start on the long grain. Pin routers are sometimes used here instead of bearing-guided tools, especially for full-thickness cuts.

BIG CUTTERS

In my view, any cutter with a diameter over 2 in. is too big for a router. And even with so many kitchens being homemade today, big cutters occupy only a small percentage of most router-bit manufacturers' inventories. They are hazardous, not only because of their sheer size, but also because of the required slower speeds. Slower speed means greater hand-feed forces, and greater forces in turn require the setup to be more secure. If you do a lot of raised panels, consider using a shaper, which has the power and durability for this type of work.

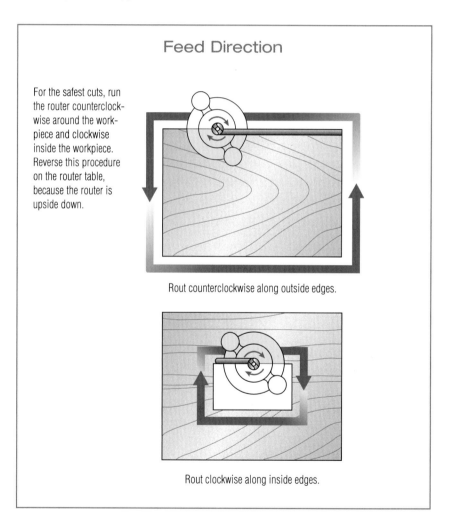

Feed Direction

For the safest cuts, run the router counterclockwise around the workpiece and clockwise inside the workpiece. Reverse this procedure on the router table, because the router is upside down.

Rout counterclockwise along outside edges.

Rout clockwise along inside edges.

Climb Cutting

The safe hand-routing feed direction should be left to right (against the cutter rotation) on the outside of the work. On an inside excavation, the feed direction should be clockwise, also against the cutter rotation. This is a good rule, but feeding against the cutter rotation usually causes some tearout. The effect is similar to chopping against the grain with a chisel while moving the chisel in the direction of the chop. It is very efficient, but the cutter can grab and tear out some stock. If the router is fed right to left, only the most recalcitrant of materials will tear out—the only real incentive to climb cut.

There is some risk in feeding with the cutter rotation; the router can self-feed. The cutter transfers its rotational force into a forward pull and tends to pull away from the work as it self-feeds. This doesn't happen with the standard cut because the operator is pushing against that force. But when you're pushing the router in the same direction as its self-feeding tendency, it's much harder to control. However, light cuts with small bits transfer very little force back into the router. Climb cutting with them is relatively safe. The bigger the cutter, the greater the power transfer. The problem also gets more serious on end-grain, where the cutters have the most traction.

On the router table, the climb cut can transfer a lot of energy into a relatively light workpiece. It's very easy to lose the work when feeding left to right. And once the workpiece starts to self-feed, your fingers can be pulled into the cutter, a disaster indeed. If you have the work in a holder that has some additional mass, the likelihood of a self-feed is reduced, and you can keep your hands safely away from the cutter. A workpiece not

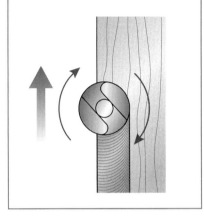

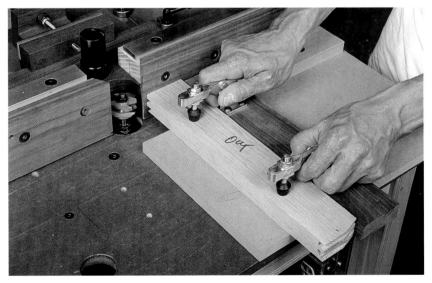

These toggles not only press the work down on fiberboard, but are comfortable enough to use as handles.

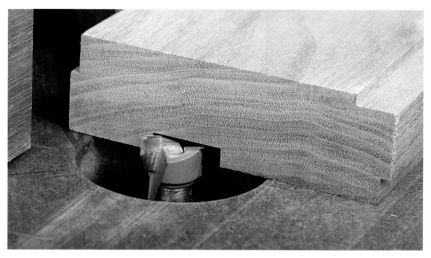

Feed the stock from left to right if widening slots on the fence side (nearest the fence). Feed from right to left if the slot is being widened on the operator's side. The initial groove should be made feeding right to left.

fixed into a holder of some sort is very hard to control when climb cutting. Climb cutting is always risky. Take very light cuts with small bits to learn about the phenomenon, and know your enemies. The self-feed of the climb cut is one of them.

THE ACCIDENTAL CLIMB CUT

Widening inside cuts (as in dadoes and slots) can be hazardous. Taking the cut on the wrong side of the pathway may result in a climb cut. Pay attention to cutter rotation (counter-clockwise on the router table) and cut against the rotation when widening tunnels. Dovetail sockets, ways, and box joints are commonly widened with specialty joinery fences.

Stock Preparation

Work that has been poorly milled will yield variable results and may self-feed or kick back unexpectedly, especially if the cutter is trapped in the work, like a slot cutter (on edges) or straight bit in a dado. There is also potential for the work to self-feed or kick back on edge cuts if the work is bowed. As the work is pressed down and relaxed on the table, it may cut more on the top or the bottom of the profile. If the bow is quite pronounced, a sudden reduction of down force may kick back the work. Crooked or poorly edged material may be the cause of unexpected self-feeding or kickback on inside cuts.

Removing a lot of material on the table may also distort a stick that started out flat and straight. This phenomenon is often seen while ripping on the table saw. The two halves of a rip often go their separate ways. Inspect your work often while table routing. If you are removing enough material to relieve stress and the work changes shape, then kickback, self-feeding, or torn cuttings can be expected.

Cutter Surprises and Risks

Router bits cut or destroy most things in their pathway even if they're dull. They can even get hot and burn you. They can also break, especially if they're small in diameter. Most of the cutting and force on a cutter at work is at the end of the bit. The lever (distance) from the end of the tool to its weakest point can be long enough to break the tool in modest working conditions: dovetail bits are notorious for this. To minimize breakage when no other cutter will do, use solid carbide or take the cut in stages with a plunge router. Also note that a sloppy setup increases the likelihood of breaking the tool. Keeping a cutter confined to its pathway helps stack the odds in your favor.

No countermeasure will prevent all accidents. Cutters break. Fortunately, cutters that break in inside cuts lose their kinetic energy quickly against the wall of the cut—and they are usually trapped there by the cover of the subbase. They are rarely dangerous. A cutter breaking along the edge of stock is a threat, but rare. I've heard horror stories, but I think you're more likely to get hit by lighting than a ballistic tool bit. I've put in thousands of hours behind routers with all sorts of cutters—new, used, experimental, unbalanced, reground, and so on—and I have never broken a cutter while edge routing. I've also chipped a lot of carbide when hitting nails, knots and embedded hardware, but I've never been hit by cutter shrapnel.

This table leg, out of square, will rout differently on the router table depending on which face is against the fence. If it is too far out of square, it could break the cutter.

This slot cutter is engaged in the work. Lift up the work while routing and anything can happen—usually what happens is not good.

THE TRAPPED CUTTER

A trapped cutter is any bit that will destroy the work if you lift the router. These include slot cutters, keyhole bits, and dovetail bits. Any of these will ruin the work if you tip or lift the router. If the cutter is in the router table and you lift the work, you'll also ruin the cut. You may also unwittingly dislodge or pull the cutter from the collet and change its cutting depth, causing both dangerous and unexpected results. There is not much you can do about this but pay attention.

OUT-OF-BALANCE CUTTERS

Bent, self-sharpened, reground, big, long, single-flute, and even ordinary cutters can be out of balance. Dirty or worn collets can send a well-balanced tool into a resonant frenzy, too. With any of the above, test the tool in a variable-speed router for vibration first. Hold the motor with both hands, with your thumb on the off switch. Accelerate a step at a time and shut the tool down the instant any vibration is felt. Operate the bit only at speeds below resonance (marked vibration) or not at all. Frankly, I would return an out-of-balance bit for a refund or replacement. Unfortunately, I have seen new cutters from most suppliers that have some vibration.

Let your collet fill up with a resinous mess from a softwood routing session and the next cutter in the collet may not be secure. Collets should be immaculate; if they're not, you'll see a loss of holding power.

Health Concerns

Routing is a dirty, dangerous, noisy business. Eye protection is essential, and goggles that won't let a chip in anywhere are cheap. Ear protection should not be overlooked. Routers are noisy, and with a vacuum they are doubly noisy. Noise suppressors safe to NRR:25 dB minimum should be worn at all times when routing, as sound-energy insults are cumulative and can lead to noise-induced hearing loss.

Every reasonable effort should be made to collect the dust and chips from a router to prevent nasal and lung damage. The router table is very easy to set up with dust collection equipment, and you should use this whenever possible. Repeated exposure to wood dust is a recognized health hazard, so you need to minimize exposure. (For more on this, see *Woodshop Dust Control* by Sandor Nagyszalanczy, The Taunton Press.)

POSTURE

Most shop furniture is too low for routing, not only for inspection of the work but for your posture. For me, the best height is around 36 in. to 38 in. high for table routing, and about 40 in. for hand routing. Select the best height using the adjustable height of the drill-press table as an experimental surface. There's no sense in stooping and tiring before you're ready to quit.

Hearing protectors, safety goggles, and dust masks help prevent long-term health damage from frequent router use.

Working with Sharp Corners

Routing can produce very sharp-cornered workpieces—sharp enough to cut your hand. Although routing with gloves can have its own hazards, I do use rubber gloves from time to time for protection. Be cautious, though. If a cutter catches a glove it can pull your hand with it, winding up the glove in a second.

Common Router Limitations

With more than 75 different routers available at any one time, their limitations sometimes seem deeply buried in all the product hype. And with some 35 router books in publication, most of the information dwells, sensibly enough, on what the tools can do. This is fine. But it's always a good idea to discuss the router's limitations as well.

Tearout is easily caused by big cuts with dull cutters in difficult wood.

Dull cutters, or even new cutters, if left to continue beyond their cutting times (time it takes to rout the cut) will burn the wood.

Risks and Problems

I've mentioned the inherent instability of routers and that they often have poor visibility because of black or opaque subbases. Routers also produce a lot of waste, foul the air, and can even ruin your hearing if you fail to use protection. Their cutters are obviously very unforgiving, and they can quickly wreck a workpiece if you lose control. They also will cause severe injury if any part of your body gets in their way.

It's also possible to break a tool bit every now and then and have a piece of metal whizzing though the air (although this is rare, since broken bits generally lose their energy rapidly against the workpiece surface). Perhaps the most common complaint against routers is their tendency to produce tearout in the workpiece. Planes, chisels, and saws have their own problems, but they don't tear like router bits do.

Routers can unexpectedly lose their depth of cut. As pointed out, the motor may slip in the casting, or the cutter can squirm in the collet (especially with dirty or worn collets, or if the tool shank has been scratched or dinged). And, of course, worn router bits can also burn wood.

PRODUCTION WORK

Nearly all of the problems mentioned above show up more frequently with higher and higher production rates. The standard 110-volt router can be overworked when made to do heavy cuts such as raised panels in near continuous-duty conditions. You shouldn't expect this production performance from a 110-volt router. Short-run, limited production can be done with two routers having similar setups. Let one tool do most of the dirty work even if the cutter is worn or chipped, and let the other router with a new tool take a finish cut. In a setup like this, you can get much more than twice the output of one router—but nothing compared to a 3-hp to 5-hp shaper.

POOR JOINERY RESULTS

Stock preparation is key. Though not actually the culprit, the router sometimes gets the blame when poor cuttings are the results of bad material preparation. The key to a good result is the idea of a "reference surface." For accurate joinery, you generally need to work with two flat surfaces: one on the workpiece and one on the machine. These reference surfaces can be on the work, template, jig, or fixture. For consistency, the work has to be free of defects, square, accurately sized, and uniform in thickness and width. To achieve consistent router joinery, therefore, you'll need standard stock preparation tools such as a table saw, jointer, and planer. You'll also need the skills to use them.

It's true, however, that cutters are sometimes out of specification due to manufacturing problems or regrinding. Usually jigs and fixtures can be adjusted to compensate as long as the error, for example, doesn't involve matching cutters such as those for cope-and-stick joinery. Even here you can sometimes compensate by nudging the setup by a few thousandths of an inch. An accurate micrometer or dial indicator will help here.

TEAROUT

Router bits tear out wood, and if you plow sideways (across the grain), you will break out the exits and entryways. Prevention is usually fairly simple, however. You'll need to clamp a sacrificial piece of scrap along the edges of the work so that, in effect, you're routing a larger piece and the tearout occurs on the scrap. All routing has the tendency to tear out the work. You'll always need appropriate strategies to minimize this phenomenon.

Cuts across the grain also raise surface tearout. Almost always, the surface tearout can be sanded away; but if the router is cutting on the top of the work, it will produce a bumpy ride and spoil the cut.

Even straightforward operations such as edge and inside cuts can tear out along a vertical surface, such as the wall of a rabbet. However, sharp cutters, light cuts, two-stage cuttings (such as a straight-bit preplow for dovetails), climb cutting, and quality wood will minimize the havoc—but it should be anticipated.

The floor of basic cuts such as rabbets and dadoes can get very "fuzzy," especially at the corners. You'll frequently find yourself reaching for a chisel or scraper to lightly clean the surface and remove the leftover fuzz.

Template Guides Smooth the Way

Cross-grain cuts tend to lift wood fiber, and consequently render a bumpy surface under the router. Using a collar guide and a template keeps the router off the work, and also provides a smoother cut.

Only the right corner will tear on this crosscut, so a spoil board clamped on the edge will prevent tearout. The cutter spins in to the work edge on the left and can't tear.

The up-spiral bit leaves a fuzzy surface.

The floor of this rabbet shows the slight swirls of the cutter tip. The wall is typically much cleaner than the bottom cut.

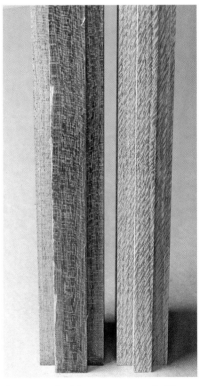

The cut on the left was pre-scored with a $\frac{1}{32}$-in. pass. The cut on the right was not.

Router-bit technology hasn't been perfected to achieve great results for that bottom portion of the cut. Router bits are designed primarily as side cutters. Consequently, the floor of many profiles may not be as sweet as the wall cut from the same tool. There isn't much you can do about this, but a light score cut ($\frac{1}{32}$ in. or so) can eliminate a lot of tearout along the floor/edge corner. Uniform feed rates commensurate with the cutting rate and chip ejection will produce the best cuts.

"Cutter zing" is the metal song you hear when a cutter is bending in its pathway. Part of the stock is cut away to show the chatter from this phenomenon.

Pattern Bits for Trimming

Try using a pattern bit with a top-mounted bearing—they're frequently larger in diameter and stiffer—instead of a flush-trim bit. The pressure on the top bearing causes less deflection. Collar guides also have the same effect.

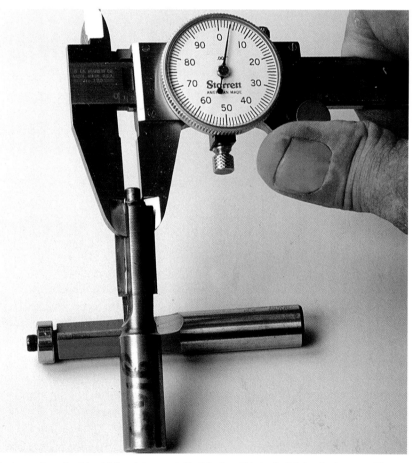

The large-diameter trim bit is a lot more inflexible than this typical ½-in. flush cutter. There is only 0.2 in. of steel left in the web of this bit.

CUTTER DEFLECTION

Router bits turning at high speed can actually deflect enough to make the cutting path wider than the bit diameter or cause unexpected chatter. Sometimes dovetail cutters and long, straight bits are just too narrow for the intended task. There isn't much you can do about this except use extremely light cuts. This will help, but the chatter from a long, narrow bit is indeed a problem. If a narrow cutter is needed, try switching to solid carbide or another flute design. There are also other solutions for narrow clearance jobs. Saws and chisels, of course, cut into very narrow pathways and should be considered if time permits (easy for me to say).

Long $\frac{1}{2}$-in.-diameter trim bits with the bearing on the bottom are common and prone to deflection because of side pressure applied to the bearing. Deflection causes chatter and can lead to a broken bit.

DEPTH ADJUSTMENT

Precise depth-of-cut mechanisms that don't require fussy setup or test cuts don't exist. If precision and accuracy are your goals, calibration cuts are essential. Everything in the metalworking industry is first calibrated and then driven on slides or ways with precision-cut screws, gauges, and readouts. But woodworking tools are not capable of precise repositioning throughout their travel. Only very expensive production tools can be "dialed" to a cut—and test cuts are still advisable. For whatever reason, woodworking power-tool adjustability is still in the dark ages. Two, three, four, or more test cuts are commonly needed to reach acceptable accuracy for a depth adjustment. Many shops use dedicated routers locked to depth for one job only rather than take the time for setup.

To be sure, precise depths are not always required for decorative cuts such as roundovers, bevels, and ogees. But they are necessary for all joinery applications such as glue joints, miter locks, and cope-and-stick work. You can't make an accurate half-lap, tenon, dovetail, box, or tongue-and-groove joint without precise depth control. This can clearly be frustrating.

Plunge routers are better than fixed-base routers for depth adjustment, but can be frustrating. They only lock onto one post and will squiggle a bit.

Backlash is a common cause of the depth-adjustment problem in rack-and-pinion systems. Porter-Cable's four pins, when passing the split in the base casting, can foul the adjustment. Bosch's two-stage fine adjustment is a step in the right direction, but it, too, has its backlash and motor slop in the base casting. The new Makita RF1101 hasn't solved the problem, either.

Gauge readouts, except for the Porter-Cable 7518, are often shamefully unreadable. The stamped rules on plunge routers, with or without magnifiers, are merely indications of depth. Don't expect to find readouts

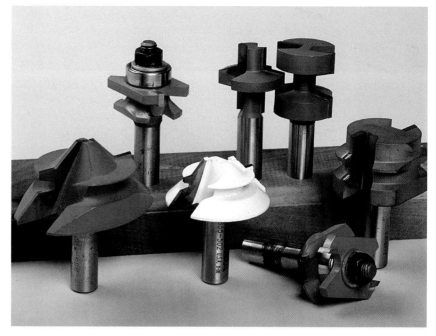

Paired and interlocking joinery cutters are very sensitive to fence and cutter height positions. On a bad day, expect 5 to 10 test cuts to set up a run of joinery.

The markings on these depth adjusters are very confusing.

close enough for joinery with any of them. DeWalt's fixed-base readout is accurate to $1/64$ in., but nearly impossible to read, and its rack-and-pinion gear reacts too quickly to adjust for small changes.

Mixing metric and English units on the same indicator only confounds the problem. Bosch and DeWalt both have nearly indecipherable indicators.

Weight and Ergonomics

Routers do the shallow-depth work of chisels, saws, molding planes, and other hand tools. Though they do the work very well, they can also be awkward to handle. They are generally ergonomically designed for basic bench work, but they can be difficult to handle due to their weight and the fact that the cutter is not a direct extension of the tool, as on a chisel or hammer head. But their adaptability makes them useful in less-than-ideal circumstances. Moreover, because the cutting tool is less than 1 percent of the machine by weight, closeness and control are compromised. A wallop of a mallet on a chisel on the "line" is a pretty straightforward exercise. But controlling the cutter pathway of a router with two opposing knobs and 10 lbs. of copper, steel and aluminum between them takes some practice. Fortunately, as with bicycling, expertise will come—but setups, jigging, and such will take time. Practice is the essence of routing and woodworking.

Starting Up the Router

Router technique and setup are quite individual. Many, if not most, woodworkers learn by trial and error, rather than from a formal course. But with millions of router owners out there, the need for training is overwhelming. Although router technique could easily fill another book, I'll make a few suggestions to help out the novice.

To do a proper routing job, you need to prepare the material, secure the work, and set up the router. The actual routing technique is straightforward, but I will describe what works for me. My technique is based on safety, efficiency, respect for the equipment and stock, and, of course, a quality result.

Preparation and Setup

Routing shouldn't be done on rough, unprepared stock. Jigs, fixtures, and router guide systems are all sensitive to the shape of your work and material preparation. Pronounced mill marks from jointers and planers, for example, will cause a bearing-guided cutter to bounce and telegraph the irregular surface into the cut. Edges that aren't square will register differently in your jigs. Joints won't fit if your work is poorly milled.

Quality woodworking requires accurate material preparation; you will need this skill to get consistent results with a router or any other tool. You must straighten, flatten, thickness-plane, and square up one edge of your material before you turn to a router. A table saw, thickness planer, and jointer do this job quickly and accurately when set up properly.

Overzealous jointing may yield too few and often bumpy cuts in the stock. A ball-bearing cutter will bounce on these mill marks and transfer imperfections to the work.

There is no reasonable substitute for preparing stock properly on the jointer.

Plugging and Unplugging

To be sure, an accidental startup while changing a cutter or motor setting can be a catastrophe. Because I sometimes change cutters 10 to 20 times a day in 5 to 10 routers, unplugging is a lot of lost time for me, so I don't do it. On the other hand, I always check the switch position and pay special attention to its location so I don't accidentally trip it. This is active and necessary safety vigilance. But for

Sears and some other power cords have red LEDs in their transparent sockets indicating they're hot. This socket also has a clamp in it that holds the plug to 30 lbs. of pull.

novice users, or those who only use the tool occasionally, I'd recommend unplugging. Also remember that plugs and sockets are not switches, and they present their own electrical hazards. Moreover, the Sears power cords I use have plug locks that require you to press the lock to release the plug. Forget that and you ruin the socket.

A power-indicating lamp on the motor head would be a great feature; but in the interim, active safety practice is your responsibility. Don't expect the government, industry, or anybody else to be answerable to your safety. If that means unplugging the tool—then do it.

Smooth Surfaces

For smoother edge cuts with a hand router, use an edge guide whenever possible instead of a ball-bearing-guided cutter. The edge guide will bridge small imperfections and prevent them from telegraphing through to the cut.

The underside of this slotting jig, shown here, has a set of stops to crowd the work on two sides and a set of toggle clamps to keep it there.

This mortising jig fastens to a beam. The two-clamp knobs go right through the bench into a set of T-nuts on the back side of the jig.

SECURING THE WORK

Clamps of all sorts will impose intense force on the work, but usually on just a small spot. For example, hand screws exert 200 lbs. to 400 lbs., I-beam Jorgensen bar clamps more than 2,000 lbs., and some forged C-clamps squeeze up to 40,000 lbs. Even so, it often takes even more than the local concentrated forces to keep the work from moving. Frequently, you'll need to fence it in as well as clamp it in place. You'll need at least two clamps to rout a workpiece that's not fenced in.

It's rarely a good idea to depend on a single clamp for a routing operation. Two is safer. Templates and fixtures not only hold the work, but they also need to be clamped down. Don't depend on an unsecured jig that can slide around the workbench as you rout. Put a couple of clamps on it, or find a way to secure it to the bench or other work support.

Double-sided tape and router mats are common work holders, but they're just not secure enough. I don't use either. Brads and hot glue are safer, but standard industry practice includes clamps, cams, fences, and crowding the work with stops. A single clamp has plenty of local force but will not prevent the work from rotating; a workpiece with two clamps is very resistant to rotation.

ROUTER SETUP

Before you set up for your first cutting operation, bring your router to the bench unplugged with its collet wrenches. For a basic fixed-base router, remove the motor from the base assembly and unscrew the locking nut on the collet. Insert at least ¾ in. of tool shank in the collet. Don't insert the bit so far that the flute fillet (shown below) is in the collet, and don't clamp down on the area where the flute starts to fade out into the cutter. If the shank bottoms out in the collet, lift it up a little (about 1/16 in.). If you use collet reducers, the grip is best when the slots in the sleeves are lined up with the slots in the collet. If your tool requires two wrenches, squeeze them in one hand to about 15 lbs. for 10-in. wrenches. Adjust the cutter depth and lock the motor.

Cutters with small cutting diameters often require some grinding into the shank, unlike large-diameter cutters of ¾ in. or more on ½-in. shanks. Don't clamp the collet on the fadeout.

Saving Knuckles

Removing a router bit with two wrenches can be hazardous to your knuckles. If you're not careful, the sudden release of the collet will catch your knuckles in a scissors-like bite as the wrenches suddenly come together. You can prevent this by using the benchtop as a second hand. Position one wrench so that it's held in place against the benchtop and press down with your open palm on the other wrench.

To ensure a good tool bit grip in the collet, squeeze a pair of wrenches in a "handshake" grip to 15 lbs. or so.

A safe cut begins with a wide stick with two clamps on it. The stick has seen at least the jointer and planer; the ¼-in. rabbet bit (cutting a ¼-in. by ¼-in. rabbet) is extended ¼ in.

Beginners should set up for a practice cut with a straight bit for a ¼-in. by ¼-in. rabbet on a workpiece clamped to the benchtop. Inspect the setup, and with the tool still unplugged, pass the router along its intended pathway. If you don't snag the wire or run into a clamp with the router, you're ready to plug it in. Rest the router on the work, but keep the cutter at least one cutter radius away from the edge. For inside cuts with a plunge router, keep the bit up in the base casting. Then start the motor and ease it into the work. Don't ram it against a bearing or stop.

The feeding motion should be steady, even graceful. Sudden lurches can cause tearout and break cutters.

This first light pass is a preview cut for me. In those first few seconds of routing, I learn how sharp the cutter is, whether I have enough power, whether I've set the cutter too deep, whether my clamps are holding, and the general dynamics of the operation.

Beginners should practice at shallow depths on scrap pieces 10 to 20 times before moving on to the work. The important points to keep in mind are quality wood, superior milling, good work lockup, tight cutter and motor, and light, steady cuts.

As a rule, edge cuts are the first things done by the novice with new routers and cutters, and they are sometimes difficult to do well. Since less than half the casting is along the edge and less than a quarter of the footprint is present at the ends, it is nearly impossible to keep the router flat. There are aftermarket oversized router plates to manage this instability. Inside cuts such as mortises and dadoes aren't as much of a problem here because the base is on solid ground all around the cut. You will, however, need a jig, edge guide, or template for inside cuts. There's always a tradeoff.

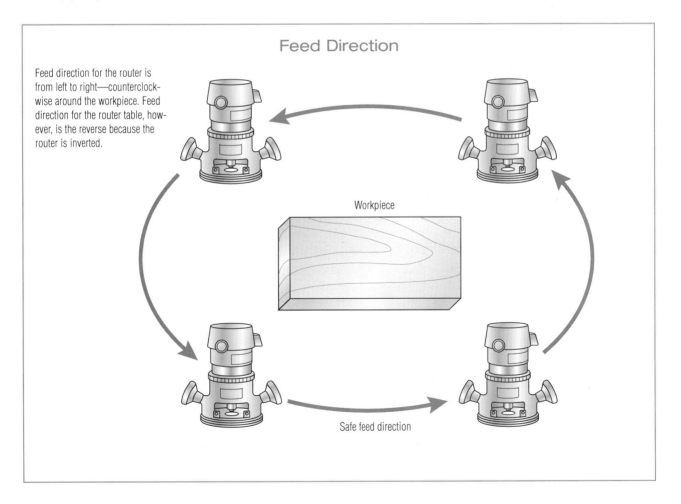

Feed Direction

Feed direction for the router is from left to right—counterclockwise around the workpiece. Feed direction for the router table, however, is the reverse because the router is inverted.

Workpiece

Safe feed direction

A straight bit is quite satisfactory for making rabbets on the router table. Close the fence down so there is 1/16 in. or so of air around the cutter. Project the cutter above the top by 1/4 in. and move the fence 1/4 in. back from the 12 o'clock position of the cutter's circle.

Always keep the work down and against the fence. Walk along with short sticks and use support rollers for long ones. These fence halves are straight, parallel to each other, square to the table, and flat. Miss any of those variables and your cuttings may be inconsistent.

Router Table Setup

The setup for the router table requires a few more steps than for a hand-held router. Again, you'll want to unplug the router. Remember that an accidental start may eject the motor pack from a fixed-base casting if you forget to tighten it before starting the router. The cutter insertion is the same. You will need to adjust the height from underneath the table—sometimes an awkward move, depending on your router. For a 1/4-in. by 1/4-in. rabbet, you'll need to position a fence and bit so that a straight bit extends exactly 1/4 in. away from the edge and 1/4 in. above the table.

Before routing, press and pull on the router fence to check its security. A fence that moves unexpectedly can ruin the work or the cutter. Table routing is very similar to ripping on the table saw—but without nearly as much kickback risk. It's easy and safe. Nevertheless, take no chances. Rout only when the process adds up safely in your mind.

Once you're ready to go, plug in the router, and feed the work evenly from right to left—the opposite of the hand-held direction because the router is inverted. Push the work down on the table against the fence and slide it steady at a rate of about 10 to 20 feet/minute. Wax the table and fence for more slip if necessary.

Template Routing

The design and making of templates is a key strategy for the effective use of routers. Templates allow you to cut virtually any shape or pattern from a simple radius to complex joinery. They are also key in achieving accuracy—a crucial skill that can't be overemphasized. The problem, if there is one, is converting your image of what the template should be into reality. Later in this chapter, I'll provide a few examples to get you thinking about the process.

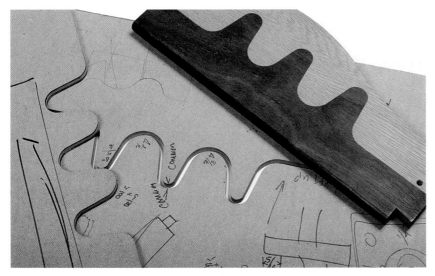

It took quite a few cutters and templates to make this tongue-and-groove sample. The process does require your attention, but none of the techniques are difficult.

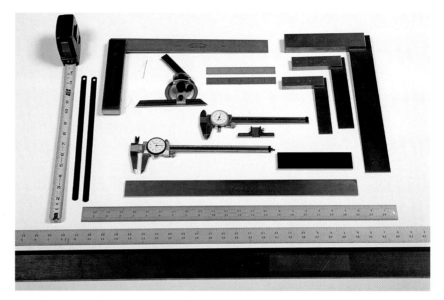

Precision rules, caliper, compass, and hardened-steel squares are necessary for close work. In addition to layout, you'll need these to isolate error, should that ever occur.

Fortunately, making the template is relatively easy. The techniques used are usually ordinary woodworking procedures—nothing fancy. In much the same way, the actual use of the template is fairly straightforward. For example, the average woodworker can master the half-blind dovetail drawer-making template jig in a few hours.

Templates for making iterated joinery (box joints, dovetails, etc.) are some of the easiest to make. Routers are the ideal tools to make these "comb" type templates. The router simply cuts one cutter width in the template material and is stepped and repeated using a block or bar to index subsequent cuts; anybody can do that. Getting the numbers to add up so that the actual cutters, bearings, and collars do their job is another matter—something we don't have space for here, either. At any rate, consistency is critical, and accurate measurement is necessary.

Templates solve many of our most complicated woodworking problems. They take much of the risk out of precarious woodworking. The accuracy allows preview of any operation on scrap stock before risking the expensive cherry, maple, or walnut on the actual project. You can run through an entire joinery sequence, for instance, from start to finish without risking any of the project stock.

Tools and Materials

Your choice of material depends on its use and to a certain extent on your skills in shaping it. Metal, plastic, fiberboards, and wood are the typical materials. Dimensional stability, transparency, expense, wear, thickness, availability, and workability all play a role in the choice. A short-run template might be best made of birch plywood or just a scrap piece of hardwood. A precision longer-run template might require plastic. Certain plastics (Lucite and Lexan) react to high-speed ball bearings skidding on them by melting. Plastic laminate will tolerate heat, but its noxious dust may be a problem. There are many factors to consider.

There's nothing fancy about the tools for making templates. You'll need a standard assortment of woodworking power tools: sanders, saws, jointer, drill press, and routers about cover it. Good layout tools are as important, though. You should have a set of machinist's rules, ground straightedges, a dial caliper, a hardened square, and a precision protractor for accurate angles. Those tools don't come cheap, but they have crossover possibilities in fine-woodworking machine-tool setup and quality control.

Template Uses and Types

One key fact is that templates can be used in a series of steps to create a surprising variety of details. I can get different types of cuts from a circle template, as well as myriad variations by changing collars, bearings, cutters, and cutter depth. First I just clamp the disk onto the work and rout the work in full thickness with a pattern bit. Then I shift the template back an inch and cut half the thickness of the work. Finally, I set the template back again and with a collar and straight bit I cut a one-diameter decorative pathway.

So, a template can be used to shape the entire workpiece in thickness, any fraction of it along an edge, or to cut a blind or through inside excavation. That much diversity is what makes the template so important.

A full-thickness flush-trimmed copy of the profile.

Shifting the template back routs a curved rabbet.

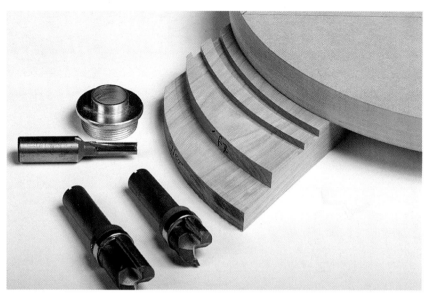

All three possibilities of the template: full thickness, fractional thickness, and the line cut.

To simplify making straight MDF templates, I usually create only one straight edge—with two ends square to the edge on the master stock. The opposite edge is bandsawn and thus never mistaken for a work edge. I always indicate the upside (work face) with a big felt-tip pen. Using opposite faces of the same template may introduce unexpected error. Because I'm using MDF, I use a machined edge as the straight edge and carefully square up the two adjacent edges on the table saw.

Making Basic Templates

A straightedge with two square corners is, in some ways, the mother of all templates. Without it, you certainly can't make much in the way of other templates. Make one as a preliminary step to making a basic comb template. (This kind of template is used for box joints and dovetails.) For stability, use MDF for the initial straightedge. Then two different pattern bits are used to make, first, a single slot that's 1⅛ in. wide. This serves as a guide to make the series of ⅝-in. slots for the comb template.

The key concept used in translating the straight template into a process is step and repeat, using an accurate method to step off the individual fingers. I use an aluminum bar to index one cut from the previous cut, thus making the series accurate to within a couple thousandths of an inch.

PROCEDURE

Before you begin, prepare the MDF materials. One is for the simple straight edge; the second is for the intermediate step; and the third is for the comb template. I use ⅜-in.-thick MDF for the first and second template, and ¾-in. for the final comb template. Whatever size you use should be a convenient size for the job at hand. I'll also have the two router bits on hand, one with a 1⅛-in. cutter and a 1⅛-in. top-mounted bearing and the other with a ⅝-in. cutter and a 1⅛-in. top-mounted bearing. (Do this in stages, with a collar guide and a plunge router. A single pass in ¾-in. MDF may break the bit.) Use bearing-guided cutters rather than collar guides to ensure exact centers. A collar guide can be off center enough to make a difference. You'll also need a piece of 1¼-in. aluminum bar stock.

First, use the simple straightedge template to make the second template with a single slot in it. Then use that to make a set of slots on regular and exact centers.

Use one of the squared-up pieces of MDF (⅜ in. thick) and rout the 1⅛-in.-wide single slot using the bearing-guided cutter. Sandwich two bearings between the two straight-edge sections to position them, and rout a single slot that's square to the face. Now use this simple slot guide to cut, step, and repeat until we get the finished comb template.

Position the slot template square to the front edge of the blank. Now with the ⅝-in.-diameter cutter, rout the series of equally spaced ⅝-in. slots.

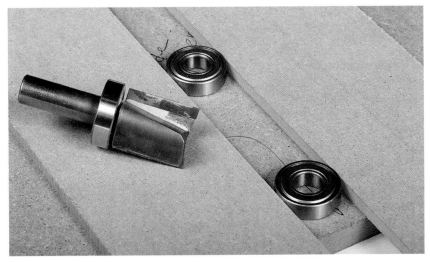

The two straight templates are clamped 1⅛ in. apart on top of the template stock used to make the comb master. The stock should be big enough so when it's clamped on the master, the router won't hit the clamps.

Use the slot template to rout the slots in the master. Keep it flush to the edge of the master for every cut.

With a 1¼-in. aluminum bar indexed against the template and a straight edge, rout a series of equally spaced slots. Remove the bar and slide the template against the clamped straight edge for each cut.

Move the template on 1¼-in. increments with the aluminum 1¼-in. bar. Care must be taken every time you make a change. If a chip should get between the spacer, if the template hangs up on some surface debris, or if you bump it, you will throw off the whole sequence, and you might as well start anew. With caution and concentration, you can make a regularly spaced original comb template that has only one-thousandth to two-thousandths of an inch of error in 1 ft. of template—without measuring.

CURVED TEMPLATE

Next, we'll make a simple curved template with a reversing radius, again using MDF stock. The central idea is to cut a disk out of MDF and use both the disk and the surrounding "hole" material as the starting material. Mounting a curved section of disk adjacent to a curved section of the "hole" creates a transition from outside to inside radius that can be useful. (Depending on how exact you need to match the radii, you may need to actually cut two disks—one with a slightly smaller radius than the other to account for the thickness of the kerf.)

First, make a disk 6 in. or so in diameter out of ⅜-in.-thick MDF. Save the hole, as it will be used to make the inside radius. Now screw the disk (or part of it) to a ½-in.-thick piece of MDF. Take a section of the "hole" template and screw it down on the MDF and up against the disk. The transition from the inside radius to the outside must be imperceptible. If you feel a bump or anything other than a smooth transition, the final template will inherit the defect.

Now with the two templates screwed to a blank, head for the bandsaw and cut off the waste, leaving ⅛ in. or less to be flush trimmed. Use a pattern bit and trim the master even with screwed-down templates. The routing, template making (disk, etc.), assembly, and bandsawing take time, but the process is easy.

Combining straight and curved sections in the same template presents no special problems. Layout and positioning are very important to the success of the template and will take some practice to master.

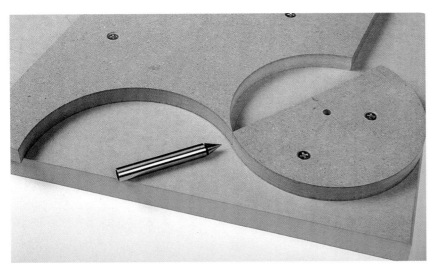

Screw the subtemplates (templates used to make the master) down on the master. The transition (pointer) must have no perceptible defects.

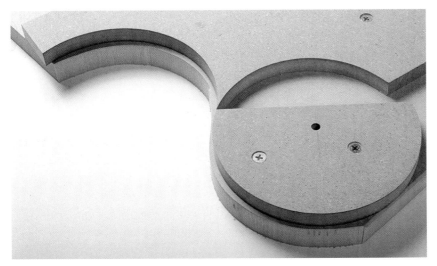

Bandsaw the waste from the template base before trimming the two layers flush.

TEMPLATES FOR A SNUG FIT

Objects with straight or curved sides can be used as "maps" to make templates and to make nests for the objects themselves, such as for French fitting. For example, you can make a snug home for a 12-in. Starrett square with a few pieces of scrap and a pattern bit. I screwed little straight-sided sections snug against the square on a ⅜-in.-thick piece of MDF. With this "window" in place around the square, I removed it and routed away the underlying MDF with a pattern bit.

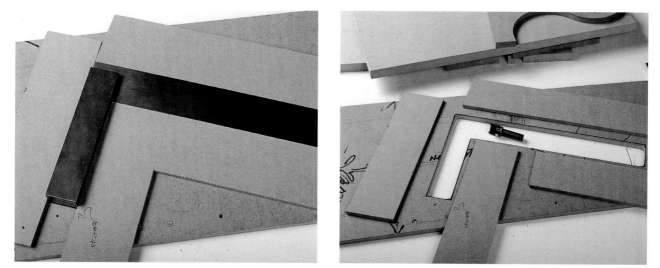

I made this window template by screwing down straight sections all around the square. Place the template wherever you want and rout out a pocket for the square. Use short pattern bits.

Screw down some straight templates around the 2x4 "map." Use a folded bill to offset the templates a little. Remove the "map" and rout to pattern with a ¾-in.-diameter pattern bit.

Rout a practice mortise through some scrap. Use a fence screwed to the bottom of the template to index the work consistently.

Now with the window template I could rout a home for the square in a drawer bottom (or whatever). Let's just repeat this procedure with an ordinary stick for a little practice, say a 2x4.

To simplify the corner fit in the final workpiece, first round over all four corners of the 2x4 with a $\frac{3}{8}$-in.-radius bit. Make the window template using a $\frac{3}{4}$-in.-diameter bit so the radii of the corners match up.

Screw down some $\frac{3}{8}$-in. straight sections of scrap around the 2x4 "map" as shown at left. Leave about 0.008 in. slop between the 2x4 and the guides.

Waste the inside of the template with a jigsaw and then flush rout even with the straight templates. Remove the scrap guides and trace the window onto the work. Jigsaw or drill out the inside waste, clamp the template in place and trim it with a flush trim bit.

Resources

Adjustable Clamp Co.
417 N. Ashland Ave.
Chicago, IL 60622-6397
(312) 666-0640
Clamps

Amana Tool Corp.
120 Carolyn Blvd.
Farmingdale, NY 11735
(800) 445-0077
Router bits

Bruss Fasteners
P.O. Box 88307
Grand Rapids, MI 49518-0307
(800) 536-0009
Steel X-dowels

CMT
P.O. Box 4185
Greensboro, NC 27404-4185
(800) CMT-Bits
Router bits

De-Sta-Co
P.O. Box 2800
Troy, MI 48007
(810) 594-5600
Toggle clamps

DeWalt Tools
701 E. Joppa Rd.
Towson, MD 21286
(800) 4-DeWalt
Electric power tools

Fein Power Tools, Inc.
3019 W. Carson St.
Pitttsburgh, PA 15204
(412) 331-2325
Electric power tools

Hampton House
200 N. Brewer St.
Greenwood, IN 46142-3605
(317) 881-8601
Katie Jig

Hitachi Power Tools
3950 Steve Reynolds Blvd.
Norcross, GA 30093
(800) 706-7337
Electric power tools

J&L Industrial Supply
P.O. Box 3359
Livonia, MI 48151-3359
(800) 521-9520
Machine tools

Jesada Tools, Inc.
310 Mears Blvd.
Oldsmar, FL 34677
(800) 531-5559
Router bits and accessories

JessEm Tool Co.
171 Robert St. East, Unit #8
Penetanguishene, ON L9M 1G9
Canada
(800) 436-6799
Rout-R-Lift

Jointech
11725 Warfield St.
San Antonio, TX 78216
(800) 619-1288
Joinery jigs and templates

Keller & Co.
1327 I St.
Petaluma, CA 94952
(800) 995-2456
Dovetail templates

Leigh Industries, Ltd.
P.O. Box 357
Port Coquitlan, BC U3C 4K6
Canada
(604) 464-2700
Dovetail and joinery jigs

Makita Tools
14930 Northam St.
La Mirada, CA 90638
(800) 4-Makita
Electric power tools

Micro Fence
11100 Cumpton St., #35
N. Hollywood, CA 91601
(818) 766-4367
Edge circle guides, ellipse maker

Milwaukee Electric Tool
13135 W. Lisbon Rd.
Brook_____ WI 53005
(262)
Elect

Porter-
Box
Jack
(80
Ro   ic
wo

PRC
73
Pa
(8
Ro

Reid
22
Mu
(80
Jig hardware

Ridge Carbide
595 New York Ave.
Lyndhurst, NJ 07071
(800) 443-0992
Regrinding of router bits

S-B Power Tool Co. (Bosch)
4300 W. Peterson Ave.
Chicago, IL 60646-5999
(877) 267-2499
Electric power tools

Taylor Design Group, Inc.
P.O. Box 810262
Dallas, TX 75381
(972) 418-4811
Incra jig

Veritas Tools, Inc.
12 East River St.
Ogdensburg, NY 13669
(800) 871-8158
Woodworking tools, router accessories

Patrick Warner
1427 Kenora St.
Escondido, CA 92027
(760) 747-2623
Acrylic offset subbases and jigs

W. L. Fuller, Inc.
P.O. Box 87677
Warwick, RI 0288
(401) 467-2900
Drilling tools

Woodhaven
501 W. 1st Ave.
Durant, IA 52747
(800) 344-6657
Router accessories

Index